FIRING ON ALL CYLINDERS

Recognizing Our Co-Responsibility for the Creation of Our Own Lives

DAVID POWER

WESTBOW
P R E S S
A DIVISION OF THOMAS NELSON

WestBow Press books may be ordered through booksellers or by contacting:

WestBow Press
A Division of Thomas Nelson
1663 Liberty Drive
Bloomington, IN 47403
www.westbowpress.com
1-(866) 928-1240

ISBN: 978-1-4497-3981-2 (hc)
ISBN: 978-1-4497-3982-9 (sc)
ISBN: 978-1-4497-3983-6 (e)
Library of Congress Control Number: 2012902233

Printed in the United States of America

WestBow Press rev. date: 05/21/2012

Table of Contents

"The art of progress is to preserve order amid change and to preserve change amid order".
Alfred North Whitehead (1861-1947)

Firing On All Cylinders

Many countless books and articles have been written over the centuries trying to guide us, prod us, and even scare us into living fuller, healthier more complete lives. They have been written by doctors, physicians, psychiatrists, health aids, spiritualist and clergy. Most of them, leaders in their respected fields and most of them with a sincere motivation to pass along their accumulated knowledge in the hopes of alleviating some of the misery surrounding the human condition we all find ourselves in. The problem with this is that their field of expertise limits them to that one aspect of life that they are most familiar with. The doctors of course will fill us with information on health and hygiene, the knowledge of disease and how to combat it or prevent it, working within his field of endeavor to strengthen our human bodies, physically. That in of itself is a good thing and advice well worth listening to.

The psychologist on the other hand is going to try to attack it in another way with the dealings of the mind. He will introduce us to all the complexities of this organ we call the brain, its phobias, its fears, its subconscious and conscious dualities, trying to instill harmony and peace in your life by regulating its functions. The pastor, priest or spiritualist is of course going to deal strictly with the etheric life force we call spirit. He will address the condition of your spiritual wellbeing and try to administer Godly advice and direction. He will lean on the word of God to help your soul and restore oneself to the grandeur of life the Lord originally set up for us, His Divine Design. All very noble all very good.

Each of these specialists are usually very well intentioned and can deliver vital information to us if we are willing to listen, but each of them is only a partial answer to a threefold problem. Man is not just a body, he is not just a mind and he is not just a spiritual being. Man's nature is three fold and until all three areas are looked at and addressed simultaneously, one area will always drag down the other leading to feelings of incompleteness and stagnation.

It may be your loftiest goal in life to seek God and follow to the best of your abilities. His spiritual lessons, your love for His word and its teachings may be the very flame or passion that fuels your life and gives you direction. Let me ask you a question, how much focus and attention can you give an area of your life with a crushing migraine that shuts you do down and leaves you suffering? How much of His Divine life is thwarted from you by chronic fatigue or listlessness. The list of ailments goes on and on.

The body has a huge impact in all the areas of our lives but especially within the spiritual sphere of oneself. You cannot attain the spiritual heights that are possible with an albatross around your neck. It also works the other way around the spiritual health of an individual has a tremendous influence on how you interpret your quality and vivaciousness of life. With a mountain of unforgiveness and a valley full of anger you will never be 100% alive. Those unchecked emotions are like spiritual vampires sucking the life right out of you. Your spirit is forever underpinning your physical and mental well-being. Look if you want to be all that you can be, feel your best at all times, it takes a holistic approach. Many of you get the proper sleep, eat the right foods and exercise continually but never feel it's totally paying off for you.

That is simply because we are ignoring one of the other main aspects of our being. There is no way around it. If you want to be the best athlete in the world or just the best softball player you must start dividing your attention to the other areas you may have ignored. We must first look at the whole of ourselves, our symbiotic selves and not just at a single aspect or all three will suffer.

St. Paul classified man into three parts, body, mind and spirit and like the cylinders of a car if one is off it will affect the whole performance. There is nothing like firing on all cylinders. It is living life to the ultimate fullness it is the way life is supposed to be lived but sadly very few ever attain it. There are many people out there that live just for the body. Their identification of themselves is solely physical and that is really sad because the body is the cruelest of all task masters and vanity is the most fleeting of partners. Many others are religious monopolies that live for the word only and leave their temples in ruins. This temple we are given is one of the greatest gifts we can have here on earth and should be treated as such. It is a marvel of engineering and unsurpassed in its complexity, but it must be maintained and properly looked after or it will fall into disrepair and hardship.

Last but not least we have the intellectuals whose only concern is the filling up of his or her mind with knowledge and learning usually ignoring both the physical and spiritual side of oneself to their own detriment. We are a symbiotic creature by nature though we don't like to admit it. We have many of these relationships throughout life in many different forms. Relationships of mutual benefit or dependence, but in this context we will define it strictly within the terms of ourselves and our spiritual relationship within.

When we finally recognize the importance of this co-dependence and set about aligning these three areas the miracle is set in motion. You unleash a power inside like you've never known before, spiritual power created ironically by a form of surrender, a bending of the knee so to speak to the realization of your co-dependence both on your Creator and His ways but also in your responsibility, your end of the bargain, to develop and nurture this ongoing relationship. A little fine tuning of this symbiotic relationship we have going on inside ourselves, this relationship between body, mind and spirit, treating its parts but knowing its wholeness. If we break it down to its basic human element, your mind and spirit cannot be at its best, if your body is sick, your mind and soul cannot be at its best, if your mind is sick, and everything suffers if your spirit is not well. Yes, many of us can still function if one or more of these areas are affected but certainly we must agree we cannot fully function, we suffer a lack, a wanting, that then permeates into all areas of our lives, leading to all types of needless chaos and suffering.

With just one good look at our society today we can see one area that without question is out of balance. We've strayed from the basics like good food and exercise to fast food and video games. Our children have gone from experiencing life first hand to living a type of voyeuristic existence thru movies and video games. In my day when we wanted to play baseball or basketball we hit the field or the court now the children of today hit the on button of the television and gaming console never leaving the room.

Video games and movies have their place. I love them myself but they must be balanced off. We must also physically experience some of these things we just take for granted. I also see a similar correlation going on within our churches today. The majority of people are quite satisfied leaving their spiritual lives and growth in the hands of their pastor or priest. They show up on Sunday wanting to be entertained, give me some stirring spiritual music, an uplifting message, and I'm all set, I've done my part. Nothing could be further from the truth. The truth is that spiritual life works on a percentage basis, whatever percent you put in is exactly what you will get back, if you put in 5 percent you will receive a 5 percent dividend in return, if it be 20 percent, 20 percent is your demonstration. Ask yourself this question what difference has your religion made in your life, in your home and in your affairs, how much peace of mind, courage or understanding has it revealed, for make no mistake real religion offers all these things and more.

(Romans 11:33) "O the depths of the riches both of the wisdom and knowledge of God how unsearchable are His judgments and His ways past finding out."

Spiritual growth is a hands on endeavor. There is no way around it. If we relegate ourselves to 1 hour a week of someone else's thoughts and views on God, how we will ever form our own. How will we know what we truly believe, how will we ever hear from God ourselves with that approach, it can't happen. We must seek, we must knock and we must answer our own doors. God wants to talk to you one on one. Your life is multifaceted and uniquely your own and you must take a hands on approach or you will never achieve its fullest fruition. When you are willing to accept and recognize the three fold nature of man, when you are willing to take the reins and responsibilities for this life that you've been given here on this earth, when you are ready to give up on this passive approach to spiritual life that so many of you now hold whether it be conscious or not, then and only then will we see miraculous changes in our lives. We as Christians are asleep at the wheel. We are satisfied with the reader's digest version of the word we receive every Sunday, letting God speak to us through our pastor or priest rather than hearing from the Almighty ourselves. It's a recipe for disaster and luke warmness.

Yes it's alright to lean on the wisdom and strength of another individual, to seek Godly council and direction but that must be balanced with a striving for self-reliance and personal strength. The natural progression of a student is to learn from the teacher and go beyond always onward, always forward, till you become the teacher and your students (your circle of influence) feed off you. You possess within yourself a power and strength which few are fully aware of. We are quick to use the crutch of others and to develop the limp that they have. Strive to be your own person, your own City on the hill. If we weren't meant to do so we would not possess the ability. But we do. Ralf Waldo Emerson one of the world's most incredible minds said that," we lie in the lap of immense intelligence which makes us organs of its activity and receivers of its truth". In his essay called Self Reliance he states "it truly demands something God like in him who has cast off the common nature of humanity and has ventured to trust himself for a task master. High be his heart, faithful his will, clear his sight, that he may in good earnest be doctrine, society, law unto himself that a simple purpose to him be as strong as iron".

Learn from every source; hear God in the wings of the wind, but most of all, for your benefit, learn to stand on your own two feet. That with the exercise of self-trust, newer powers shall appear a new respect for the divinity in man and a revolution within your soul. Sing a new song, your own song, renovate your life. Never worry about being misunderstood or scoffed at for you will find yourself in tremendous company, Socrates, Plato, Newton, Galileo were all misunderstood. Jesus Christ Himself was the most misunderstood. To be great is to be misunderstood and remember greatness always seems to appeal to the future. Be a pioneer for yourself and don't just tread water or tread the same ground as others. Your potential is immense and you will never be satisfied till you blaze your own trail. Couple yourself with your inner presence of God and what you forge you will not forge alone and will have everlasting implications for you and all of those around you. Philosopher Arthur Schopenhauer once wrote; "all truth passes through three stages. First it is outright ridiculed. Second it is violently opposed. Thirdly it is accepted as being self-evident". God's truth always becomes self-evident, the process is seldom easy but it is always worth the cost. Remember your potential is limitless. The possibility of a thousand forests is contained in a single acorn. Our Lord thru nature expresses His abundance and limitless potential everywhere.

One tree in one season produces thousands of acorns. Of the thousands only hundreds take root, of the hundreds only a few live to maturity replacing the parent and continuing on, but over the life of the tree limitless blessings and growth is its potential. This reflection of God we see in nature is also fully present in each one of us, for our soul is much like the acorn; the possibility of a thousand blessings is contained within each soul. For the fruit of the tree is seed, the fruit of the soul is blessings in all its shapes and forms.

If there is a thousand forests in a single acorn think what unlimited potential is within one soul. Can we get an Amen for that? Jesus said and I quote, "It is done unto you as you believe". Your final chapters in your life will be written by your own hand or it will never be written at all. There are no other authors of your life but yourself. When we lift up our eyes to the infinite impulse of spirit, the supremacy of mind and the wonders of human existence we become balanced and buoyant, bathed in the light of Christ, this inner radiance dissolves anything that is not divinely inspired; it eliminates all appearance lack, loss or disease. Limitation is no longer part of your vocabulary, then and only then do we fire on all cylinders.

Relevant Christianity

Before we can precede any further we must reach a point of commonality or agreement upon what authority or source we use to gain our knowledge or wisdom. Which rudder will guide our boat? In practical Christianity we must bend our knee and unify ourselves to the teachings of our master Jesus Christ and to the supremacy of the Bible in the dissemination of spiritual truth and guidance. No matter how you may regard Him or classify Him Jesus Christ is easily the most important and influential figure to ever grace this planet. His life and death and the teachings attributed to Him have influenced the course of human history more than any other who has ever lived. More people's lives have been influenced by His doctrine than the culmination of all human understanding combined.

Jesus holds this distinction for He gave us the only perfect statement of the Truth. Truth of the nature of God and man, the truth of life and of the world and most importantly the relationships which exist between them. He gives us practical methods for the development of our souls, the unfolding and shaping of our lives and circumstances into the things we really wish them to be. He teaches us the meaning of life and death, what the nature of God is and what our own nature's consist of, why we become sick, impoverished, but most importantly how to overcome these evils and bring true ever- lasting prosperity into our rough and tumble lives.

He teaches that man is essentially Divine and eternal and that we are only punished by our own mistakes and may rectify things with our righteous thinking and action. He teaches no specific system of theology or religion and the whole tone of His mentality is definitely anti-ecclesiastical. He seemed almost at war with the religious officials of His day whose pretensions to authority as the representatives of God He completely laid aside. He taught principles only and insisted upon a certain spirit in our conduct. He discouraged hard and fast rules knowing that the letter killeth but the spirit groweth life.

He clearly teaches that the time has come when man must make each and every day a spiritual Sabbath by knowing and doing all things in a spiritual light. The depth and magnitude of His teachings are unsurpassed elevating him truly as the Savior of the world. Jesus showed humanity what can happen when someone lives their life as though God were real to him and that love is the ultimate power, the ultimate force in this universe.

Commonality-Bible

Look at everything as though you were looking at it for the first time or the last time. Then your time on earth will be filled with glory. (Betty Smith, American author (1896-1972)

We must all come to recognize that the Bible is an unfailing way for us to work within the spiritual laws of the universe. It is an introduction to God, and how His universe works. A human owner's manual. It possesses history, biography, poetry and song. It contains some of the world's greatest literature and powerful parables. Many of its characters live on today in books and plays and sermons of all kinds. Its influence is incomparable and undeniable.

In order to build a sturdy house one that is to survive the wind and rain and protect us from all that is outside we must place that house on a firm foundation on a rock. We have undoubtedly heard this analogy many times before and we repeat it here for there is simply no better illustration to be had. We need not have volumes of knowledge endured by many hours of Bible readings and study but what we must have is total faith in it. It must be our Rosetta stone unlocking the mysteries of this life which is both physical in the human sense and spiritual in the Godly realm, symbiotic at its essence.

We live balanced on a razors edge between the two. We must appreciate the fact that the Bible is the most precious and authentic of all man's possessions. It is a combination of inspired documents written by all different kinds of men in all different kinds of circumstances over thousands of years of time. These documents though seldom originals and seldom are the actual writers known for certain, are an inexhaustible resource of truth, a spiritual vortex as you will allowing us a glimpse into the very mind of God Himself. When asked the inevitable question who wrote the Bible the answer is clear.

Divine wisdom is its author and that is that. The name of any particular writer of any of its particular books is irrelevant. The path by which it has reached its present form does not matter. It employs history, biography, poetry and other various mediums to evoke its message, once revealed cannot be hid. It has moments of literalism and moments of interpretation. It is a tapestry of man's ascent to God woven for us and given to us in a spirit of love, and its pages should be worn and tattered.

Sometimes it seems that the Bible tries to teach things that seem to be contrary to common sense and rational thinking. That is simply because many of its stories were taken for literal statements of fact when in essence they were merely parables used to convey spiritual and metaphysical truths. Parables are employed in the Bible for they are the best at cutting through things like time, social status and geography and allow everyone the privilege of illumination on their own terms. Jesus perfected the art of the parable and used it extensively thru His ministry. He knew human nature as no other ever did and taught that strength, true strength came from the inside not the outside. He is the very template of what we are to become. Joseph Pulitzer (1847-1911) eloquently sums up a parable when he wrote "Put it before them briefly so they will listen, clearly so they will appreciate it, picturesquely so they will remember it and above all accurately so they will be guided by its light".

Jesus by the age of twelve had a commanding knowledge of the scriptures so much so that He confounded the very scholars of His day with His interpretation of the Word. He is quoted as saying I have not come to destroy the Word as many of you presume but I have come to fulfill it. Jesus came to bring those very words to life, to live them, not just to hear them, or to read them, but to truly live them, and that is precisely what He did.

He loved the Word and so should you. If it was good enough to be used by Jesus, to be treasured by Him, it's good enough for me. Let nothing keep you from indulging yourself on the meat of the word; cry out for inspiration and understanding and realize what you are holding in your hands isn't just a book but a living organism of life, a spiritual vortex when correctly divided adds up to sweet victory in your life and potentially all those around you.

To the person that has been spiritually awakened by the word of God nothing is too good to be true. For those that use the Bible regularly and with understanding will experience a real change of soul, a "born againness". An opening of one's eyes and a new freshness about life that is hard to define. It is the change of soul that matters. The mere accumulation of fresh knowledge received intellectually makes no appreciable advance in the soul. The Bible is especially designed to bring genuine change about and when it is regularly courted and used, it invariably does so.

Mankind is very prone to classify things. They love to categorize, segregate and put things in nice little boxes. We have colors to define race, social classes to define monetary status, schools to divide intelligence. We have short, tall, fat and skinny, we have quiet, loud, and abrasive, we're Americans, Canadians and Mexicans, and we have single, married and divorced and the list of variations go on and on.

All this divisiveness we use to alienate ourselves from one another is laid to rest with just two words, two words from the mouth of Christ to set many on the true path of human evolution and spiritual development. Those two words are the first two words of the Lord's Prayer and they are "Our Father".

In one fell swoop Our Father lays bare the true commonality we have as a people that we are all the children of one Father, that we are all on equal footing in the eyes of the Lord. He has no favorites, no superior or chosen race, he is an equal opportunity employer and this misconception of superiority, which lies at the root of all racial injustice, just melts away with the spoken words of Christ. Our Father, nine letters, nine letters tears open the raw truth of the brotherhood of man, we are all of one family, we are all connected within the matrix of thought and consciousness we call the heart and mind of God. We are not just close but a connected part of one another, to the point of hurting someone else, in any way, shape, or form is only hurting oneself. Helen Keller once said, "There is no king that has not had a slave among his ancestors, and no slave who has not had a king among his".

We must as both individuals and as a people have a true concern for the spiritual condition of our own individual soul and the strength of our relationship with God. There is neither Jew nor Greek, there is neither bond or free, there is neither chosen nor not chosen. That makes you and only you responsible for your life's condition, deep down we all truly realize that there is no one else to blame for where we are in life, yet on the flip side this same reality gives you the freedom by working within the frame work that the Creator has set up to rectify any situation and bring a little heaven into one's life.

The whole key as simple as it sounds is simply to work with God. To submit a little bit, step aside a little for a short time and give Him the controls. He gives us the ability to alter and direct our lives. The free will to do anything, anything at all, good or bad, but with this freedom comes consequence. Jesus declared, "We reap what we sow". That is no pious platitude, it's a spiritual law imposed on everyone like it or not and we must take them seriously. These spiritual laws work on you whether you believe in them or not.

Justly we must recognize the responsibility we have toward one another, "no man is an island". Being sparks but from one flame we are all connected on many levels we are but limbs from one body. When Christ stated "I and my Father are one" He is eluding to the oneness He had found within, His deep connection to the Father sustained by prayer. He lived within His presence giving birth to the scripture, "I live, move and have my being in Him". He thought His thoughts, He knew His will. He was completely attuned. Someday we will be like that as a people; a connectedness in the mind and a consciousness sharing of everything.

Body

Who am I? What am I? Where did I come from? Questions of the ages, asked a million times by a million different people, replied a million times with a million different answers. Who to trust? What to believe?

To the question of who am I? I can't tell you who you are that is a lifelong quest for yourself but I can certainly tell you who you are not. You are not your body. You are not this vessel with arms and legs that gets you from point A to point B that is purely your physical identification. On this plane you are not that reflection you see in the mirror every morning. You the real you are not subject to bumps and bruises, sickness and disease as it would seem to appear; the real you is Spirit, beyond our comprehension and human understanding, never born, never to die. A physical manifestation of being an individualization of life and of energy and of movement within Him our Creator our Father.

We cannot see Spirit we can see only the manifestation of spirit, when it is clothed in being, in form, and in flesh. The real you is the spiritual substance underlying and sustaining every activity of the body. This body is our vehicle on this physical plane, being symbiotic creatures with synergistic relationships we rely on each individual element of us to create a harmony of existence. The body is certainly the least when seeking an order of importance but its duties and functions are paramount for a complete and harmonious life. A life that radiates, a life of inspiration, a life full of peace and goodness, love and wisdom. One in which I know that today and every day I'm drawing into my experience a measure of truth a measure of beauty and a measure of harmony. I know my body is a miraculous instrument upon which life's essence plays out my song. Psalm (13; 6) "I will sing unto the Lord, because he has dealt bountifully with me".

This wonderful thing we call life simply put is housed within the body, and for that reason alone we must give it our highest regard and consideration. Some things we can take for granted our health should not be one of them.

Years ago the old adage, that health is as natural as sunshine as right as rain was pretty close to a truth. Maintaining a balanced life usually meant good health, it wasn't something you had to try hard for it just sort of happened. Today though things are different the assault on the body isn't just from our self-indulgences and sinful ways, it's from our very own societies and our very own environments.

Today major corporations bottom line, their insatiable level of greed has led to the contamination of our water supplies (chlorine, fluoride) the polluting of our air, the desecration of a food supply or diet, the prostituting of our medical fields, and a numbing complacency among Gods people as almost half of their lives are stolen from them as they pass on at ages 60, 70, 80. Outside the shadow of what we call advancement and civilization many pockets of people live to the ripe old age of 100 and beyond, most of them of sound mind and active lifestyles, and in terms of longevity and quality of life they have us trumped hands down. Simple diets, simple lifestyles lead to simple amazing lifespans. Is it an anomaly, a freak of nature, I think not for back in Genesis (6; 3) the Lord sets our lifespans at one hundred and twenty years and that is its potential? We are the ones that exponentially shorten it. When we fail to take into account our three-fold nature, when we allow ourselves to ignore or abuse any one of these prime areas (body, mind or spirit) it leads us to the paths of destruction and into the valley of the dry bones. It certainly can be avoided and even better yet corrected if need be for the good Lord always leaves us a way out. He always leaves a door open.

Man thru his ignorance and greed has polluted his environment and in turn polluted himself. We eat and drink to our hearts content but everything is tainted. I do not want to sound like a prophet of doom and negativity but it is true. We must be made aware. We are what we eat. We become that which we put in our bodies both physically and mentally and unless we are eating organically grown fruits and vegetables, range fed beef, and drinking filtered, spring or purified water we are going to have problems.

Problems not so much brought on by ourselves for we all certainly need to eat and drink but problems left at our doorstep by an agricultural industry solely concerned with producing vast quantities of processed foods for an ever increasing population.

Take our fruits and vegetables today, they are grown in chemically fertilized soil and then sprayed with insecticides, that beautifully looking apple may look and taste great but comes with a price, that wonderful steak you had last night is beef that was irradiated and feed steroids and growth hormones long before the supermarket and that glistening glass of water has both chlorine and fluoride as its active ingredients.

The very air we breathe unless you live very far from the city is laced with more airborne pollutant then I care to name, even our oxygen is being leeched out of the air. 150 years ago the oxygen content of the atmosphere was around 38% to 40 % percent. Today in many cities around the world the levels are at 18% to 20% almost a 50% drop considering the fact that at 6% oxygen levels all of us suffocates and die.

All this contamination is propagated upon us without a fight. We just accept things and go on saying it's just the way it is. What's one more rain forest or one less species? Not to go off on a tangent here but these rainforests that are being cleared at an alarming rate are literally the earth's lungs which are being torn out of her. The agriculturist will say "we need the trees, we need the cleared farmlands". We as a people should be screaming WE NEED TO BREATHE!

All of this affects our lives and our bodies much more than we give credit too. Progress calls it better living thru chemistry but the end result of our commercial growing is a nation that is nutritionally starving to death. We are not emancipated in that sense to the contrary 66% of Americans are overweight to the point of obesity, but at the same time we are literally undernourished and poisoned by our food and air.

Food is supposed to deliver to us vital nutrients, vitamins, minerals, enzymes, amino and fatty acids. We eat to acquire these nutrients and when our bodies don't get them from the processed food that is our diet, we naturally eat more. What a vicious cycle. This situation is dire and I haven't even touched on fast food, MSG, and Trans fats that are slowly being forced off the markets.

As of this writing Trans fats used in cooking everything from donuts to French fries are being taken off the market. Ever wonder where they came from. In 1912 we used this funny little substance from nature called butter to cook our foods. It was naturally delicious, it wasn't health food, but it did the trick. Then a company called Crisco Foods came up with a product called what else "Crisco".

The company discredited butter saying it was bad for you but that its product "Crisco" was actually good for you, an industry was born at the expense of a nation's health. Low and behold almost 100 years later we find out that this substance turns into an almost plastic like consistency within, that our bodies have a very difficult time eliminating. This is a perfect example of why we must take the condition of our health very personally. Not often can you trust advertisers and large companies. Trust yourself, and let common sense be your guide.

That is just a little bit of the diet aspect. We have many more things today working against us, and the health of our bodies, many of us are overworked, over stressed and over spent and that's not taking into account what our minds do to us with our warped thinking and neurosis, which we will take up later in the chapters on the mind. If we are not aware of what's going on around us we will suffer. Ignorance is not bliss in this case but there is always room for hope. The Lord always leaves us a way out. We are His creation and considered His children. He willingly gives us the keys to the kingdom if we will only receive them, and those keys open the door to a land of dominion and the home of strength, poise and health.

Preventive Maintenance

It was the summer of 1977, I was in my third year of high school and life simply put was a whirlwind. Anyone who has already been there, and that would probably include you, knows what I mean. It was a year of firsts for me, first real job, first real girlfriend, and first real whiffs at adulthood. What a time in anyone young life but the superseding thought on my mind was my first car and my driver's license. Now I had arrived. I was looking freedom and adulthood right down the barrel and I will never forget the first time I laid my eyes upon my first car. I couldn't believe it. No amount of pinching myself could bring me back to reality. I could focus on nothing else except my red 1976 Chevy Camaro Super Sport. Eight cylinders of pure bombastic power just sitting there in my driveway. Revving that engine was more fun than any rollercoaster or trial bike I had ever been on, and cruising with my friends dominated that summer. Freedom and power all wrapped up in this glistening chariot of a car. It ran like a dream and I was in my glory. As in any teenage utopia this one had a beginning and an end. Six months into owning my new car it was giving me trouble. On the outside it was as beautiful as ever, shining red paint I would wax until my arms would fall off and mirror like chrome I could check my look out in, but on the inside something bad was happening. Something ominous was on the horizon. My car became increasingly difficult to start, it would stutter and stall at red lights and the ferocious power it had at the beginning seemed to fade and wane. I was devastated so

I took my baby as any concerned parent would to the doctor. The doctor in this case was a truck mechanic at a local garage and after a few hours of tinkering and swearing he gave me the diagnosis. Mike was his name and he walked toward me with a half-eaten half smoked monster of a cigar protruding from his mouth. How he could even speak with that thing between his lips was beyond me. It sort of reminded me of a broken windshield wiper with a voice, and that voice told me, son you have two completely fried cylinders in that engine. You once had eight but now the car is only running on six, you've lost 25 percent of your engines capabilities and if you continue to drive it the strain you are putting on the remaining cylinders will eventually blow the engine entirely. Either you repair it now or your car will be toast in no time.

It was decision time, do I shell out the eight hundred bucks, that I don't have, to repair the car or do I continue to drive it knowing somewhere down the line I would be doing further damage and possibly ruining the car completely. That's the decision many of us are at in our lives right now. Many of us are not running on all cylinders, we continue on for we must but we know something is not quite right and the scariest of all is knowing that if we remain on that same road that same path we will do ourselves further damage and short circuit all the good things we were placed here to attain.

Our Lord created us and oh what a marvel we are. We are the very co-mingling of flesh and deity. Perfectly manifested in the vestige of Jesus Christ. It's His heritage miraculously passed down to us. To all those with ears to hear and eyes to see. St. Paul correctly classifies man and divides him up in three parts, namely; body, mind and soul. The three cylinders to your human engine. When any one of these three areas is out of alignment, it creates an imbalance that then impedes on the other two. Often times it can be very subtle and lie undetected for a long time, but like the car we see and feel warning signs. Getting a grasp on how we are wired, man's three fold division, do we begin to see the truth about the nature of man? With truth comes power. Jesus said, and you will hear me repeat this a thousand times. "I have been given the ability to bring heaven down here on earth". Jesus possessing this ability only means we possess it. We possess it. Where? In cylinder shaft number three we find our souls. Watch out if you get this cylinder firing correctly for of the three its importance has no rival. Harmony, place, vitality and joy, all that it takes to bring a little heaven into your existence flows from this cylinder, and very often it's the most ignored and neglected. We will focus on the role the soul or spirit plays in this symbiotic dance in later chapters for now the focus is the body and that is cylinder number one.

Often times when discussing with a believer about the deteriorating condition of his or her body they love to throw at me the Pauline verse that states, "physical exercise profited little", now I have to believe that while Paul was penning such words he must have spilled his coffee in his lap, or broke his quill, or ran out of ink, for something compelled him to stop midstream in his thinking for he failed to finish the statement he was introducing. What he had to have meant was physical exercise profited little compared to the glorious knowledge of the spirit. With that I can concur for nothing can compare with the wealth of spiritual gain available through Gods word present in the Bible. The Bible is a portal leading one on a path of unsurpassed wisdom and power, without it human beings as a race stand no chance. For the spirit the Bible has no match or equal and is to be revered as more precious than gold or silver. Building a strong spirit with fortitude and perseverance is the greatest favor you could ever do yourself. Creating a strong mind that cannot be tossed to and fro ranks a distant second. The body in this hierarchy ranks last but is still crucial to living a complete life while living on this plane. All three divisions are permeated and intertwined so closely that to focus on just one or two of these aspects are reckless. Listen just like the car running with two burnt cylinders, you may still be able to navigate the hills of life but why put yourself at such a disadvantage. Why make it so hard on oneself. He gave us three cylinders for a reason. Running with all three pistons pumping, hills aren't even hills, they are little bumps in the road you look back and laugh at. What was so laborious or difficult becomes simple and easy as we function the way our Creator intended us to. No more swimming upstream rather we allow the Lord's current to carry us to where we need to be. Life is to be a joyous and exhilarating ride, but how many of us truly feel this way. How many of us are broken down by the side of the road waiting for our rescue to arrive, not even knowing what step to take next. What you need is a tow truck called dominion and dominion is what we have been promised. Break out the tools you may need to acquire it, for it is you who must seek, it is you who must knock, and it is you who must open the door to all that is available and all that is promised.

Prayer As Preventive Maintenance

If I were to ask you the question, a half hour a day of what specific daily regimen will keep the body fit and free from sickness and disease? I can see the hands raised and I'll bet if I could pick you, you would answer exercise. Exercise is key to maintaining a flexible healthy body but it is not the key. The key resides in the higher truth and the higher truth is we heal ourselves most effectively from the inside out, not the outside in. Exercising one's body, ones temple is imperative. Physical fitness is the proverbial fountain of youth but no amount of exercise, as valuable as it is will prevent all diseases. No amount of exercise will prevent a virus from invading your body. There is only one function that you can do that will accomplish this, and that is therapeutic prayer.

This ½ hour a day spent in meditation and in the presence of God will not only ward off much of the sickness and discomfort we deal with now, but it will center your whole life automatically. It will do more for you than anything you could possibly imagine or do on your own and I will repeat this at the beginning of any practical steps, you take, when speaking of the mind, or the spirit.

If you were to have to choose between a ½ hour a day in deep communicative prayer or a ½ hour a day of exercise, prayer wins hands down. Truth is there is no choosing between the two because both must be implemented in your life. Both are vital. Both are keys to complete living. When firing on all cylinders your immune system goes through the roof. It functions on an extremely high level. It functions how it is supposed to function. It can protect us from all the maladies this world has to offer. Prayer truly is preventive maintenance for your body. Emerson said, "Prayer is the proclamation of a joyful and beholding soul" and Alexis Carrel wrote "only in prayer do we achieve that complete and harmonious assembly of body, mind, and spirit which gives the frail human reed it's unshakeable strength".

In prayer we recognize the Truth. The Truth is He has given us divine health right from birth. He created us perfectly. The world would like you to believe that sickness and disease is a natural part of this earthly life. It's the earthly condition, and so we must resign ourselves to the fact. Just because a majority of the people suffer from excessive sickness and disease doesn't mean that this is the way it's supposed to be. It just shows you the extent of the misconception purveyed on the human race. Weakness is ingrained in us right from the start rather than the Truth. Psalm 50:12 "The world is mine, and the fullness there of". The "fullness there of ", is not only material objects of great price, but the immaterial ones that are priceless, that no amount of gold or silver could buy. Things such as peace of mind and perfect health, the appreciation of a sunny day or a wonderful partner to spend that day with, all these positive things and many more are the "fullness there of".

You laugh and say perfect health, right, I suffer daily from migraines you laugh and say perfect health tell that to my arthritic joints, or the forty extra pounds draped all over me.

Perfect you say, I don't just have one ailment I have too many to count. They call me chronic. You scream in pain and with an undercurrent of anger and say thank Him for that. I don't think so. I didn't say thank God for your maladies, I said to thank Him for the Divine Health He originally gave you not what you have allowed yourself to become. There are no migraines, phobias or rheumatoid arthritis in Gods way of doing things. We are placed above this, but the world in general doesn't see it this way. It seems satisfied to float along in the tide of human misery believing what its eyes see, rather than what the spirit teaches, that it is "goodness and mercy that shall follow me all the days of my life". Psalm 23:6.

Jesus wasn't sick a single day of His life and prayer was the cornerstone of His existence. Listen I hesitate to even call it prayer for the word has been clichéd to death, call it a half hour therapy session with the best trainer, psychologist, spiritualist that money can't buy.

A therapy session started off with just thankfulness for all that you still have and a removal of negativity and doubt and limitation in my life. God is good only, perfect only. Today I open my eyes differently, wider, and look out upon a broader and newer horizon, for all the experiences I have had that were limited or unpleasant I now see the glimmer of a new dawn. I now allow every sense of depression or heaviness to depart from me and let my soul be lifted up to that Divine Presence which resides within me.

Letting go of limitation I now enter into a larger concept of life. Releasing all doubt I embrace faith, knowing that every form of doubt and fear is seeing only in part. I open my spiritual eyes fully to that which is whole. Limitation, doubt, fear, sickness slip away from my experience as I turn and acknowledge that which is greater.

Today I open my eyes and mind to the breath, and the height, and the depth of life and being that is God, to all the possibilities encompassed within. 1 Corinthian 13;(9-10) "But when that which is perfect has come then that which is in part shall be done away with". Allow that which is perfect (God) to come into your life, give him more reign. Visit Him and actually speak to Him. 1 John 3; 1 "Behold what manner of love the Father hast bestowed upon us, that we should be called the sons of God". With just 30 minutes a day you can experience the wholeness of God because you are a son or daughter of the Most High. Do we really appreciate what that statement means! Thru prayer we can experience more and more of that life that abundant life that was meant for you. Wholesomeness, love, health all the fruits of the Spirit, waiting to be picked by you off that wonderful Tree of Life we have growing right inside us.

All this miraculous change takes place with just a half hour a day given over to Him in meditation and prayer. Literally speaking a ½ hour a day spent in prayer, in His presence, is Life. Sit and enjoy, sit and partake, sit and be well, enter into your daily inheritance, your daily bread. Anne Frank wrote in her diary about prayer "How wonderful it is that nobody need wait a single moment before starting to improve the world." Nobody does. We can do much more on our knees than we ever could do on our feet. It's in the secret place of the Most High where the miracles occur.

I completely believe that from my conscious dwelling with the Most High there will be projected into my life a concrete manifestation of all my needs: be it a healing or be it a physical necessity, that within me, Spirit sees, knows, and understands, all my longings, all my desires. Ephesians 4:23 "Be ye renewed in the spirit of your mind", allow this rejuvenation, like a blanket of snow to pour forth and cover you with a newness of life, a freshness, a captivating whiff of Divine Life.

Life that never ceases even at physical death it continues on ever seeking its Creator. Have you ever pondered the depths of the word Life, all its implications and meanings? Take a few moments and ponder the words God is Life. God does not just give life or just arbitrarily create it, He is it. He is that intangible life essence found in all living things from plants to birds to you and me.

This life force experienced here on earth is what links us all into not just the brotherhood of man but also all of nature, and the universe. If we look deep enough it's not hard to see God expressed as life all around us. It is everywhere. Sit down in your field or yard and just look. The grass you are sitting on is alive and growing right under your butt. In the grass is a cacophony of activity with all types of insects and bugs acting out their parts in this symphony of life.

The soil houses, the roots or fingers of all these plant forms from weeds to trees, and in the soil itself everything from worms, to microbes, set up shop for another day. Life is totally blanketed all around you, hence God's wide brush strokes on this canvas called earth: and God Himself said when He was done creating it, that it wasn't just good, it was "very good".

God is Life the Creator of all, and life is His creative substance like a potter with a lump of clay, God works life itself into His statues and artworks making life the productive element of all.

God as life, in the creative activity of life, takes this productive element and molds it into what we call being. Being is the conscious awareness of ourselves, and that being, that preciousness of life itself is temporarily housed within this earthly flesh we call body.

Being and Spirit are interchangeable words, being pardon the pun one in the same. This is how your earthly body becomes the temple of the living God. Do we recognize this life force this power within as the Father of your being. If not it is this lack of understanding or inappreciation that is the cause of all want and lack. When we accept and realize that this Spirit this Being flows thru every atom of my body vitalizing and invigorating renewing me and every part of my physical existence.

That this pattern of perfection which is God operating thru every organ, every function of my human body and that this conscious inter action thru prayer allows me to possess the very vitality of the Infinite. It allows me to say with true conviction, I am strong and I am well. I will continue to be strong and well. Its power is my power its strength is my strength. Every breath I draw is a breath of perfection-born of spirit made manifest thru me.

James 5:15 "and the prayer of faith shall save the sick and the Lord shall raise him up". You must understand one thing. These Bible verses are not just pretty little poetic words used to prove a point or paint a picture, they are "pillars of truth". They are "universal laws" that govern this human existence. They work within the percentage of faith or belief you put in them, but remember one way or another they always work. Consciously or unconsciously, Gods law is always working itself out in your life so work with it rather than against it and remember a ½ hour a day just keeping in touch with the Lord will transform your life top to bottom.

Back To The Garden Of Eden

Our bodies were created to know no sickness. They were created to know no death. In our original form we knew no sin and communed directly with the Almighty Himself, we were ordained to have dominion over everything in this life and to uniquely reflect His love, glory and holiness. We are the pinnacle of God's creation here on earth and were called upon to be fruitful and multiply. That was the original plan and it was a good one.

We must strip away everything we've learned, (man's wisdom) and return to the original blueprint for our lives, (Gods wisdom). Health, Happiness and Prosperity are as natural as the sunshine. It is man's non recognition of his original relationship with God, it is man's forgetfulness of the power within and of the source of His very existence that makes him look beneath himself to the natural side of life instead of the spiritual, and tries to measure his souls value or life's worth by intellectual or financial pursuits or some standard of right and wrong, hence forth he has no true foundation to build upon. Without the cornerstone of Truth all man made edifices must crumble.

Man grows and develops by his enfoldment from within. He lives from within all his faculties are cultivated from within. His God is embedded within. We have within us a spiritual force that is ever active a power that needs careful attention that we don't misdirect or wrongfully use or worst of all, not use at all. Recognition of the Spirit within leaves us ready at an instant for use by God.

Returning to the Genesis of life we cannot be sick. Living in harmony with the Spirit frees us with love and goodwill toward all. Anxiety and worry do not exist in the garden. They were weeded out alongside the fear and hatred and all the other indigenous overgrowth.

Youngevity Verses Longevity

An awakened soul is one that is in intimate contact with its Creator and enlightened to all its possibilities. That's another one of the greatest gifts given to man and each soul grows through giving expression to the light that it receives.

As human beings we are given another gift of almost equal value in pertaining to our earthly existence, Health. A healthy body produces a vibrant and vivacious existence. The vitality, the wisdom, the peace of God is mine, and I revel in His fullness of life.

Yes, health is a gift that is bountifully bestowed upon all those willing to receive it. It is a gift given that allows us to live this life to its utmost fullness. It allows us to renew our vigor, remakes our strength, heal our bodies and bring peace to our hearts. It is a dynamic force empowering us to be all that we can be. So why then in today's society of hustle and bustle do so many of us completely ignore this treasure at hand and instead seemingly do almost everything in their power to destroy it. To rend it null and void in pursuit of some other shiny brass ring, twinkling before our eyes, be it money, position or power. Not until this the most precious of gifts, health is lost, do we pine away at what we once had and grasp blindly at anything to regain it once again. Only then do we realize its true worth, its pricelessness, and only then it's sometimes too late.

It has been almost 4 years since my step-father Mr. Robert Selby passed away. From an educational and business standpoint Bob was a brilliant man. Schooled in both the sciences and philosophy he was the kind of guy you could ask almost anything, on any topic, and he almost always had the right answer. He was uncanny with a tremendous reservoir of knowledge and life experience. He was also an astute businessman and entrepreneur, by his early 50's was able to retire to a very comfortable oceanfront lifestyle in South Florida. One of the only chinks in his armor was in his approach or attitude toward his physical body. He didn't have one he did not fire on all cylinders. He ate what he wanted, drank what he wanted and exercise was nonexistent. Physicality was just not him. He did not consider his body to be a temple, with maintenance, or his health a gift to appreciate, so when the doctors discovered a blocked artery in his neck he figured they would just go in, operate and fix it. During the operation however he suffered a major stroke. It took 4 months of rehabilitation in that same hospital before he was even allowed back home; but of course, physically and mentally he was only a shell of the man we once knew. Bob once sharp as a tack was now relegated to a leather armchair and afternoons of Wheel of Fortune, and The Price is Right.

Toward the latter end of his life, a poor health care worker was brought in to help my mother with the heavy lifting and continuous care needed in living out his now arduous and confined existence. Through his work he gained financial success and was surrounded by the finer things in life, but inside I knew he would have given everything he had to possess the health and strength he once knew. Frustration ruled at this point and he realized that his poor health care worker was a much wealthier man than he. This man who had absolutely nothing as far as material possessions went whistled when he walked, he had a bounce in his step and a song on his lips for he possessed the priceless. Priceless for Bob wasn't a precious stone or rare piece of artwork priceless became a simple walk on the beach or even the act of feeding himself. We all want a long life, but what good is long life in an incapacitated state. Long-life or length of days is a promise given in many of the

Psalms for the man that seeks after God. We must combine longevity with youngevity (yes I know youngevity is not a word) or we could be subjecting ourselves to something akin to a prison sentence. Appreciate and thank God every day for your vitality and health, don't chase after anything be it money, power or position, at the expense of your priceless health; for ironically it seems when you finally attain what you have been killing yourself for, you will either not be able to enjoy it fully one way or another or you will be bequeathing it to your loved ones. Treat the body like the precious jewel it is, realize its utmost importance, take it down and dust it off every once in a while. Go out and even have some fun with it here and there, you would be amazed at the things it can do. Cultivate longevity along with youngevity in your diet, and exercise routine for without health and the freedom that goes with it, money is worthless.

Great good comes to the soul illumined with God's love and wisdom. He has no fear and sees no limits. He lives above the worldly plane and finds his true source of being contained within himself, his indwelling presence of Christ. He walks the earth in eternal youth for he lives in God, moves in God and has His being in him. He is like a young plant or sprout ever flexible and bending in the right directions. He does not stiffen with age but remains ever pliable in the hands of God, combining youngevity with longevity and his length of days, he finds wisdom. In his heart of hearts he sings the lines from the classic 60's song. "I was so much older then; I am younger than that now". He fulfills the original destiny of his human body and combines longevity with youngevity and lives life full, unto his last breath. He is undoubtedly firing on all cylinders.

Exercise: If you are ruled by mind you are a king, if by body a slave.-Roman historian; Cato (234 B.C.-149 B.C.)

We have learned that physical exercise and the body is rated lowest of importance compared to either the mental aspect or spiritual aspect of life. We have learned that working from the inside out is the higher truth in healing and living, but this higher truth does not circumvent the role or relevance that physicality plays in our little symbiotic dance of human existence.

We must not belittle or abandon the physical realm. In terms of humanity and the material body there is no greater gift than health, vivaciousness, and fullness of life.

Have we ever tried to accomplish something even the most simplest of things, when we are sick or run down. It makes the task 10 times harder or even impossible to accomplish. Many of us run on 60% to 70% of our capacity due to feelings of ill health or fatigue caused by our negligence of our body's needs. Instead of providing its needs we fill our bodies with medications both prescribed and over the counter. It seems man's only answer to this dilemma is always in a pill. Wrong!

We consume energy drinks as if energy is contained within aluminum cans. We diet ourselves to death and in the end hurt ourselves more than help. We are a society that simply treats symptoms rather their causes. It has made the pharmaceutical companies and their stock holders millions but has emptied us of our God given health and money. We must not just medicate to cover up our symptoms; we must peel back this onion of life and get to the core of the problem. One of those main problems is the lack of physical exercise we give our bodies.

Ponce De Leon travelled the world looking for the fountain of youth. He never found it, he never found it because as usual he was looking in all the wrong places. Physical exercise is the fountain of youth and it is found everywhere. It is found in the gyms, on the play yards, it is contained within the pools and lakes and forests and the hills. It's on bicycles paths and foot paths, it's in basket balls and baseballs and hockey pucks.

It was actually contained on Ponce de Leon's boat anytime he walked the yardarm or hoisted a sail. When he was exploring all those islands it was over flowing in all the walks and rummaging around he did, as he was looking, he was in the midst of it, and so are we.

Physical exercise contains within itself the very Holy Grail of Health and youth and there is no way around it, don't buy into all the ads on TV telling you, you can lose 50 pounds by taking this pill or program or if you need energy, drink this concoction or that potion.

Health is as free and natural as the sunshine. It can't be bought for it is freely given to all those willing to partake. Invigorating energy is created not purchased, created by you, for you and it never runs out. Physical exercise creates more energy for you down the line. Listen the energy you have at this moment is energy you have created for yourself earlier. How you feel today is a byproduct of your yesterdays.

Energy begets energy it is a universal law. Jesus said you reap what you sow; with what measure you give out you get back. Energy is a part of that equation. Energy is a self-sustaining entity that never runs out, you don't possess it, you create it, and you simply tap into its unlimitlessness.

James Joyce once wrote," I am tomorrow, or some future day, what I establish today. I am today what I established yesterday, or some previous day.

Society today is fundamentally different than in the days of our fore fathers, to live just 100 years ago was a hands on experience, we use to use our legs and a funny thing called walking to get around, we didn't go to the supermarket for food we grew it ourselves in our own gardens, we washed our own clothes in wash buckets or streams and almost everything back then had some sort of physicality attached to it. To live was to exercise.

Today every task we can think of has a piece of equipment to make it easier. Washers and dryers, cars and trucks, power drills and chain saws all alleviating the drudgery of such work by removing the exertion it once took to do them. Now I'm not saying I want to cut a tree down with an axe, I have a 24 inch, 3 horsepower Husqvarna chainsaw that will do it in a tenth of the time. I'm just giving examples of how exercise has been removed from our lives with modern mechanization. 100 years ago there was not a gym on every corner because you simply didn't need them. Today however you most certainly do.

Today we must build into our lives a time to work out and exercise. We must build and bend and stretch these muscles or lose them. It wasn't so much a need in days past as it is now. A little bit of the time we save with these devices must be appropriated to the maintenance of the physical body. Let me ask you, would you rather go mountain biking or build a stone wall around your property. Would you rather go snow skiing or shovel your entire property out with a little wooden plank? Today's day and age does have its perks.

Exercise does not have to be egregious or boring, but it must be done, and I am not here to design any one a workout routine or schedule. Each person who reads this is unique, and has their own unique set of circumstances and abilities but that doesn't exclude anyone from the responsibility of maintains one's body. Personally as an athletic individual I am ever amazed at the strength and coordination possessed within my body all that it can do and take never ceases to mystify me. I'm a firm believer in some sort of strength training in correlation with a cardio workout.

With resistance training and weights I still have the body and reflexes I had in my twenties even though I'm in my fifties. I don't live in the gym or obsessively work out. I have a routine I do at home every other day for 45 minutes that works for me and you must find one that works for you. Be diligent be disciplined and be consistent and you will be amply rewarded. Just as in spirituality exercise also works on a percentage basis, you get back only that in which you put in, you truly reap what you sow.

I could dedicate an entire book to the benefits of exercise or you could read one of the hundreds of other books out there that are much more in depth on the subject, but instead let us agree we need to unify and not divide the body, mind and soul. The whole being needs to be fed, bread meat and exercise for the body, knowledge and wisdom for the mind, and atmosphere and consciousness for the soul. Never want or lack but continue on firing on all cylinders.

Mind (Consciousness)

Ralph Waldo Emerson; "We are all organs of the Infinite" Yes we are all organs of the Infinite and that organ is the mind.

The Great Discovery Awaits

Many tremendous discoveries lay undisturbed for years and years before someone kicks over the proverbial stone and finds them sitting right where they have always been. The tremendous good and advancement that these discoveries would purvey on mankind just wastes away, year after year, century after century, with no one to mine them and unlock their treasures. We have seen it throughout the ages. Imagine the phenomenal leap mankind would have made technically had someone in the day of Moses stumbled upon electricity. Electricity was a reality in the days of Moses, it was all around them yet they knew it not. They had no one to harvest it, to control it, to make it do our bidding and so man struggled on for centuries in the dark waiting for the day, for the light to go on in someone's mind and discover this tremendous force harnessed by nature. We couldn't even imagine what life would be like today had that discovery not been made.

What other tremendous forces of nature are out there, waiting for their day of discovery, natural forces, yet unknown that will catapult us forward in our human evolution on this incredible planet we call home. There is one that is available now to the few, elite people willing to listen, willing to learn, having an ear to hear, and an open mind. One that will alter and change one's life to a degree they never would have dreamed possible. It is the harnessing and the focusing of one's mind and the use and control of one's thoughts. Until we understand the power of self-mastery, self-control and learn to direct this incredible creative energy we have within, (spirit), we live only half a life and it's the weaker half at best. Listen this is not mind over matter I am speaking of, this is mind, coupled with spirit, teamed with God, trumping over circumstances that do matter. We should never resign ourselves to anything less than the harmony that the Lord has intended for you and though contrary to popular belief we must realize life is not ruled by chaos. The mind is the great orchestrator of life it is the channel for self-expression and is the way God manifests His being within. We are not speaking of the brain in general, for that is a physical organ of the body, but the indescribable workings of the indescribable mind, your consciousness. Man has made incredible inroads into of the workings of our psyches but in reality we have really only scratched the surface. Doctors scratch around in the dark with eyes half open trying to gain some insight into its workings. Much of what they discover is debatable and is suspect which is sad because we have an infallible resource which most modern doctors simply ignore, the teachings of Jesus. Jesus Christ is by far the most incredible, spot on therapist ever born. He knows the human mind or the psyche like no one else. When we seek him and absorb his teachings we fulfill Philippians 2; 5 which says, "Let this mind be in you, which was also in Christ Jesus". We are individualized expressions of the Mind of Christ.

Jesus Christ and His teachings on the (heart) another word for mind are all we need to guide us through this maniacal maze of life. His teaching over two thousand years ago is cutting edge still today because it is Truth. Jesus teachings are the only perfect statement of Truth. The truth of the nature of God and man, his relationship to this life and the rest of the world, he has given us concrete practical methods for the development of our souls. He taught the "law of being" which is whatever happens to you, whatever encompasses you, will be in accordance to your thinking your consciousness and nothing else. What is present in your consciousness will be brought forth into your life, and what is not won't. This outer world of circumstance conforms itself to your inner world of thought. As the lord and masters of our own thoughts we become the authors and shapers of our own environments. We do not always receive that which we pray and hope for, but we do get that which we justly deserve. We do not always attract that which we want but receive that in which we are. As progressive beings we are where we are in life that we may learn that we may grow. We must learn the spiritual lesson that each set of circumstances has for us, conquer them and move on to the next, in doing so we will notice that the alteration in our circumstances will be in the exact ratio to our altered thinking. Circumstances are simply the means by which the soul receives its own. Suffering and misfortune are always the product of erroneous thinking in some direction, and it is the indicator that we are out of harmony with ourselves and our indwelling spirit. Something within one of our three cylinders is amiss. Suffering is the purification process, the removal of the dross from the gold and in most cases it burns. We come into our own as spiritual beings when we stop the whining and crying over our lot in life, and diligently search for the seemingly hidden justice which rudders our existence. When we radically alter our thinking in a positive sense when we bend are knee toward the Lord in thought, we will be astonished at the rapid transformation it will have on the material conditions of our surroundings.

Life is a foreign language; all men mispronounce it. (Morley 1890-1957)

At the core of each human being is the Creator, Genius of the Cosmos, God Himself housed within, yet we seem to live in complete ignorance to this fact. We are part of a great unfolding of Spirit in flesh, a slow but tremendous evolution of humanity, an emerging of our true spiritual heritage that contradicts much of what we see and hear today in society and simple life in general. Instead we live as crippled, limited versions of whom and what we really are. We allow our thinking to lapse into negative habitual patterns, once rooted are hard to change. We ply our minds with emotional plagues and toxic thoughts and our world mirrors this perfectly. Our minds give us a way out, our minds can give us the passion for new possibilities and higher purpose, our minds correctly orchestrated with the deeper teachings of our Lord and Master Jesus Christ unleash a treasure trove of spiritual psychology that will truly revolutionize ones entire life from top to bottom. If you are reading this you have been beckoned, you have been called and your time is at hand. Jesus teaches us to be recreated through the renewing of our minds, the renewing of our thinking and innermost thoughts and gives clear and precise, very practical directions to the building of this new and exciting dynamic, spirit filled life. Ernest Dimnet a French priest and author put it perfectly when he said "The happiness of most people is not ruined by great catastrophe or fatal error, but by the repetition of slowly destructive little things". Yes slowly destructive little things like thoughts.

Jesus teaches that our lives and all its intricacies are but merely a blank canvas that our minds are the artists and our thoughts are the brush strokes. We have been given the ability to create what we want, to have dominion over circumstance and that the whole outer world is amenable to man's thoughts. All of our life's experiences are but the outer expression of our inner beliefs and thinking. With our own minds we depict life that is peaceful or stormy, filled with satisfaction or frustration, bright or dark. We have been given free will but our free will lies entirely in our choice of thought. This creation, this rule of law acts upon us whether we realize this fact or not. There is no suffering for another man's sins but the reaping of a harvest we ourselves have sown. Accepting this truth is the first step but until it is implemented in our lives we cannot truly possess it. The greatest discovery of all time, the Holy Grail if you will, is still just out of reach; glimmering off in the distance like the shining brass ring on the ever commencing merry go round of life. When we discover within ourselves the miraculous Laws associated with thought we become the Conscious Master. We begin to direct our energies, align our intellects to worthwhile pursuits and issues. We realize that we obtain Gods favor not by chance or by folly but as natural result of continuous effort to align ourselves with God like thinking. We must understand our salvation is freely given but the responsibility for the direction of our lives is totally up to us.

This is the time, you are the person and practical Christianity taught by the Master can help us do it. God would not create man and leave him in bondage. The seed of freedom "corrected thinking" planted and watered today will quickly yield its harvest of true salvation and God ordained victory in life. Henry David Thoreau once said "Heaven is not just up above it is right here below our feet" and Jesus reiterated with "The kingdom of God is at hand". The kingdom of God is in your hand right now. Open your palm and see the keys to the kingdom within. Life should contain both harmony and a certain level of excitement and passion. There will be seeking and there will be satisfaction. There is nothing to lose and only certain gain when one couples himself with the Creator. The will of God for us always means newer and brighter experience, greater opportunity and life more abundant. It means firing on all cylinders.

Brain

Housed within the protected walls of your cranial skull lies the miracle of all miracles. Mankind's most amazing device the human brain. This goes without saying. The brain itself is an orbed fleshy organ made up of different regions or lobes that correspond to each and every different bodily function. Its complexity is so far beyond us, trying to describe it is useless. It uses neuropath ways and synapses to route different messages each with specific purposes, its scope and breadth is almost to the infinite. It is responsible for both the nature and the quantity of all bodily secretions and controls all the unconscious bodily functions we need to survive on a day to day basis. It is an engineering marvel and can and will produce within itself all that is required for its welfare and maintenance. That is its physical function and it fills out its responsibility incredibly well.

Mind

Conscious-Subconscious

Much like our spirit (that divine spark placed within you) that is entwined within this human body, our minds or our stream of thoughts are entwined within this human brain using it much like the spirit does with our bodies, as vehicles as a means to an end. Vehicles that propel us onward and forward thru this great lesson of life. The teachings on this subject are voluminous so we will try to keep things quite simple for our purpose here today. Your mind or your psyche is what constitutes your personality here on earth. Your psyche is the person we know, be it studious or inattentive, reasonable or unreasonable, your psyche or mind defines you as a person. The psyche exist in two separate divisions we know as the conscious and the sub-conscious mind with the subconscious entailing approximately 90% of the whole compound with only about 10% for the conscious aspect. Much like the icebergs seen floating in the oceans of the north, what you can see poking out above the water (the conscious side) is a little speck compared to its great mass that is underneath the waves invisible to the eyes (subconscious).

The conscious mind possesses the ability of reasoning, awareness and common sense. It uses the bodies five senses to connect and inform itself of the physical world all around it, though its job is of utmost importance, it turns out to be only a minute fraction of the whole psyche. By far the greater portion is the subconscious which has the ability to impress all kinds of suggestions good and bad upon the conscious mind. The subconscious mind has a larger and different role altogether from its counterpart. First of all it builds and rebuilds the physical body constantly in accordance with the pattern it holds for it. It governs all such function as digestion, circulation, secretions of all body fluids, breathing, rhythm and elimination. It does so without you ever knowing all these processes are going on. It can produce anything that the body requires. This unawareness can sometimes hurt us, for while we try to address a bad issue or habit we might want to break, we mainly just use our conscious mind and sheer will power, while the subconscious mind with its immense influence is pushing us in the opposite direction. Guess who's going to win. It takes aligning the two, consciously, to break bad habits such as drug addiction; or smoking. The subconscious also has perfect memory, anything you have ever seen, heard or experienced even as a child is meticulously recorded. If a person suffers a near death experience often times their entire lives flash before their eyes giving evidence to this incredible phenomena. Many people believe that all our minds are connected on the subconscious level, that there is a race mind aspect of life that very few are aware of. We as children of the Most High have been given the ability to reach out to God in prayer and share His mind. We can become as one, His thoughts become our thoughts, "in Him we live, move and have our being". The race mind is a collective of every thought ever conceived, both good and bad. In the depths of our sub consciousness we have all this information inside of us acting on us sometimes in a subverted way. We can be influenced and affected by this unconscious sharing of ideas both good and bad, sort of like a radio receiver which can be tuned to receive either positive or negative impressions. We will speak on this later; suffice to say that many of the beliefs we have in common as a race, as a people, come from this race mind or consciousness we all share.

Thoughts Are Things

Thoughts are not the wispy little clouds that float above your head like the ones you see in cartoons. The ones that seem to dissipate very quickly like a vapor in the wind. That is whimsical thinking because often times they can be more like concrete anchors tied at your waist, constricting and afflicting everything you do. Jesus's teachings and influence on the power of thought and the role it plays in your life was so completely revolutionary for his time you knew it was from God. Statements such as Romans 12-2 "Be ye transformed by the renewing of your mind", nine little words that say it all. There is no briefer or more power packed statement than this. When you study Paul's writings on the inner workings of man you can only walk away with the conviction that the hand of the Lord was upon him. Paul possessed the Christ consciousness available to us all. His words were Christ's words, his thoughts were Christ thoughts. Paul did not shy away or mince words what so ever. He didn't pretty up things or hide away his own human faults. He laid it all out bare for all to see. Paul wrote what the Spirit provided for him and it was a ground breaking look into men's hearts, and inner motives. Paul is living proof of the dramatic change that takes place in one's heart and mind, and life when one clothes himself in the Christ consciousness. Paul went from persecutor to pursuer, from detractor to defender. His inspirational writings prove the awakening of an incredible soul, a soul that found the true source of wisdom within and gave expression in word to that light he received.

"Be ye transformed by the renewing of the mind". No one was more transformed than Paul and no one had more of a right to shout those words of life from the rooftops and high places than he. And he did. There was no stopping Paul. He would later write in Romans 8:5-8 "for they that are after the flesh, do mind the things of the flesh, but they that are after the Spirit the things of the Spirit". He is asking point blank "where is your mind at"? "For to be carnally minded is death". That is pretty strongly worded and it's meant to be. "But to be spiritually minded is life and peace". This is wisdom stripped down to its absolute brilliance and simplicity. Your whole life be it a good one or a bad one revolves around one simple thing. Where is your mind at? Proverbs 23:7 "As a man thinketh in his heart (mind) so is he", another piercing piece of analytical scripture going right to the heart of the matter. When we discover within ourselves these God ordained laws of thought we become the conscious Master and work in unison with His law rather than against it. We do this by consciously letting go of feelings such as rage and anger no matter how justified we feel in them, we entertain no feelings of fear, we recognize them for what they are poisons and toxins to the body and we clothe ourselves with the mind of Christ and realize we do have the choice. Your sovereign freewill we hear about all the time is this right to choose. Listen in the measure or proportion you master (your thoughts) rather than being controlled by them that is the measure or proportion you will have in mastering your outer affairs and circumstances. No doubt, no fear, no anxiety marred Jesus's expression of love and kindness. The difference between savior and a sinner is this; the savior is the one who has perfect control of all his thought forces, the sinner is dominated and controlled by them. Be a conscious master and power, strength, and joy will radiate from you without any effort on your part. Even a very small victory in self-mastery adds greatly to one's power and those who succeed in greater measure find themselves in possession of wisdom, strength and peace. Think good thoughts and they will actualize in your life. Think bad and I think you get the message. It sounds trivial but believe me it's not. Too simplistic, capricious, that's the beauty of it. 'As a man thinketh, so he is". Seven words better yet 20 letters, sums up the greatest advice anyone could ever give you in this lifetime.

Paul's searing psychology proved his intimate knowledge of man and his inner working long before it became an arm of the medical world. Psychology today is still only scratching the surface, poking around in the dark, if you will, while Jesus' teachings if you study them expose the world as it really is. It is a mental universe, and thinking is its language. Jesus the Master knew that if mankind could master his own thought he could mold his own character and create his own environment and destiny. Jesus knew we can make or break ourselves by the right choices and correct application of thought. This is the dominion the Bible speaks of. We as a race of people never came to dominance on this earth because of brute strength as many perceive, for if that were the case the lion, tiger, and bear would rule. No it was our minds that set us apart, our thinking made us different. Always has and always will. The attributes of the mind, in conjunction with spirit make man master of his domain. Genesis 1:28 Gods very first promise to mankind is to be fruitful and multiply, replenish the earth and subdue it, and to have dominion. He gives us the ability, let's all invoke it.

Jesus with his teachings also dispels the myth of providence. Bad luck, good luck there is no such thing. Circumstances don't just happen but it is us that birth them into our lives. Rich or poor, loved or hated, healthy or diseased, all are created by ourselves for ourselves by the direction and fashioning of our thoughts to either positive and fruitful issues, or embracing the world's bestial and selfish side. Peace of mind, poise, joy, health does not come to us by chance or folly, but are the natural result of continual effort. By right choices and the correct application of thought we ascend, by the abuse and self-centeredness of thought we descend. The recognition of the role of thought is paramount in one's life because it's thought that precedes every action. Thought therefore becomes the creative cause of everything in your life. We are forever "pulling the strings ourselves" but rarely do we know it. Knowing this deep down at the very center of your being is one of the keys to a God centered life. Applying it and cultivating it is solely your responsibility but when done with pure hearts and motives we make swift and rapid progress. We are not creatures of outside conditions but masters of our own environments. God has given us dominion in the world but very few actually show it. We must put away aimlessness and weakness and begin to think with a higher purpose. Our very thoughts are alive with power correctly used we become higher and stronger. We become conscious users of our divine power. Jesus said "Fear not little flock it is your Fathers great pleasure to give you the keys to the Kingdom. It should be our great pleasure to accept them and use them for all their worth. What are the keys to the Kingdom? All the wondrous things money can't buy health, love, and peace of mind. How do we attain these things? Correct application of thought. Scripture says "Knock and the door shall be open for you". Forget knocking just use the key God gave you and let your-self in for the Kingdom of God is at hand.

Regeneration

The most fatal illusion is the settled point of view. Since life is growth and motion, a fixed point of view kills anyone who has one. (Brooks Atkinson, journalist (1894-1984)

The ability to grow younger and to reverse the debilitating effects of old age and misuse of the body. To be able to renew, re-fresh and re-invigorate oneself back to God's original process of life, being bright, being radiant, and to halt the depreciation of one's own being. Is it even possible, is it even relevant, or is it just a pipe dream spouted out by prosperity preachers and fitness fanatics pushing their own personal agendas? If there is a paradise placed on earth its right here in America, right here under our noses. The vast majority of ordinary Americans live a pretty stable, pretty secure existence yet it seems our bodies depreciate faster here than in other parts of the world. Our lifestyles (which seem to be simply the amassing of the most money possible at any cost), our diets, and our lack of exercise, all are contributing factors. As of this writing a large European study released its data proving that muscle tissue could be recovered and regenerated even after it a had been in a atrophied state for years. They took 85 year old subjects that were retired for over 15 years and living very sedate lifestyles and introduced them to mild exercise and strength training. In no time their quality of life, their vigor, and mental attentiveness was remarkably increased. These are the same people told by well-intentioned doctors and family to 'take it easy now' and to 'slow down because you are getting up there in age. PBS even more recently devoted an entire show dealing with the subject of Alzheimer's disease. It was incredibly well done and informative and it concluded the only know treatment in affect today to help stave off the effects of Alzheimer's on the general public was exercise. It showed that exercise although it could not cure it or completely stop its advance could significantly slow down its timetable. It is all very encouraging but the ability to regenerate? Please.

To find out we must trace mankind back thru the Bible back to the days before Noah. In these days human lifespan was measured in the hundreds of years and the oldest recorded living human being was the Biblical character Methuselah. He lived a life span of over 8 centuries which in those days was not unheard of. I know it is hard to believe, especially today, but just keep in mind that time can be irrelevant. We are locked in time, not God. Our universe is over 14 billion years old by our standards and God himself is infinite. Time is a human concept and very difficult to see past, but if our Creator wanted His creation to have a thousand year lifespan, I see it as no problem for Him, but alas in ancient Old Testament days though the body lasted longer the mind was ever set on evil. People with elongated life spans had more time to incline themselves to evil thoughts and ways rather than growing in the spirit. Hence the great flood and a revamping of how things would proceed on from that point in history. Hence-forth man the slow learner that he is was limited to a potential life span of 120 years. That seems high by today's standards, but that is only because we like the Old Testament saints still haven't learned. We still abuse our bodies, sully our minds, and ignore our spirits calling.

We do not see that life's infinite powers are stored away within us that all things are possible, only waiting patiently to be brought forth. We are not ordinary beings. Still we predominately cleave to the humanistic side of life rather than evolving spiritually into the higher beings God created us to be. When we awaken to ourselves we will find that we are not human beings down on earth having a spiritual experience but we our spiritual beings down here having a human experience. We are sons and daughters of the Most High making us primarily spiritual. To live predominantly in the human realm we go about our own business weakened by the non-recognition of our spiritual side and fall headlong into the snares of this world. Money, pleasure, worldly comforts, those are our gods, that is what we seek after, and sadly that is where our hearts are. There is nothing wrong with money, unless it gets loved, nothing wrong with pleasure, unless it's always self-seeking, nothing wrong with worldly comforts unless they were attained unscrupulously. Man's non-recognition of his spiritual power within has made him look beneath himself to the material side of life and tries to measure his or her value by earthly gain or intellectual pursuits, he has tried to adjust himself to circumstances, rather than realizing he has the power to adjust circumstances to himself.

In Charles Dickens a Christmas Carol there is a stunning scene where the recently deceased Jacob Marley visits Ebenezer Scrooge. He pleads with him to repent of his ways and to change his view of people and life in general. Jacob is weighted down and in agony by a colossal chain he himself is fettered to. He must drag this albatross around everywhere he goes. He screams at a bewildered Ebenezer, "I wear the chains I forged in life, made it link by link and yard by yard, I girded it on of my own free will". Revisit the scene if you get the chance for it contains some powerful symbolism of exactly what we do to ourselves, our bodies, thru our lifetime here on earth. Those chains are not just meant for the after-life, for in life as in death we shackle ourselves link by link with all our erroneous choices. When we hold on to anger and unforgiveness we add a new link. When selfishness rules over charity we add one more. When the pursuit of money, food or addiction rules our lives we are firing up the forges and adding to it daily but contrary to popular belief this chain will affect you in this present day and not only in the "here and after".

You will drag this invisible weight around with you in the disguise of disease, poverty, and loneliness. It will be with you everywhere you go, and once again a human life is snuffed out prematurely long before its intended time.

Every promise in the Bible is real. Every promise He makes He fulfills perfectly. God cannot say one thing and do another. Just because those Promises don't seem to materialize in your life doesn't make them counterfeit. He is perfection. He is infallible. If His promises are not coming to fruition in your life it is because you are somehow attacking it at the wrong angle. You are asking amiss. We don't beg or grovel to God for answered prayer; we don't plead with teary eyes and hope He hears us. We know. We have confidence. We know it is His greatest pleasure to answer our needs as any parent derives joy and satisfaction from loving their child, for what man when asked by his son or daughter for bread would give him a stone. Jesus gives us the key to every promise made to man by our Creator. It is so simple that almost everyone misses it without fail. Jesus says, "It is done unto you as you believe. I'll repeat that. It is done unto you as you believe. In whatever proportion you take His word at heart that is what you will receive back. Whatever percentage of yourself you earnestly give Him that will be your dividend, your return. You must embody His word. Absorb it. Become it. It is not enough to say, I know God is love, I know God is health, He is joy but these characteristics must be embodied by you and then brought out in yourself. For every lack in your life there is a corresponding characteristic within God that once you have embodied within yourself, you will never suffer from that lack again. You will have total freedom from it and total victory over it, never to deal with again. Lonely, find a circumstance and be a friend, money troubles, learn to give from your heart without regret or looking for reward, and so on, and so forth. Don't just be "ye hearers of the Word "but embody it and bring it forth.

Believe as a little child would, fully without doubt and a brand new world can open up for you a world of unlimited possibility. God makes no idle statements, He says what He means, do you have enough belief to match it and secure those promises for yourself, or will you just go with the ebb and tide of humanity, being tossed to and fro like a ragdoll in the current.

Pray these words with me and etch them in your heart. The joy of life circulates thru me, invigorates and fills me with trust. I let go of any fear of age or decline and know with sure knowledge that I am forever growing better and stronger, I give thanks each day for my perfect health. My body is my temple and my house is in order. The Spirit of the Most High is my spirit and His words are my words, they shall be sent forth, they shall accomplish, and they shall prosper me. My word is a tower of strength; my word is the word of God.

Exodus 24 thru 26 states "Thou shall not bow down to their gods, nor serve them, nor do after their works but shall utterly overthrow them and break down their images, and ye shall serve the Lord your God and He shall bless thy bread, and thy water and I will take sickness away from the midst of thee. None shall lose thy young nor be barren in the land and the number of thy days I will fulfill. Thou shall not bow down to their gods nor serve them."

Their gods in this context can mean anything that separates or distances you from your own indwelling spirit. That can mean food, if you are choosing that as comfort rather than God, it can be any type of drug addiction or dependency on anything other than the seed of the Lord inside you. False gods or sin come in infinite shapes and sizes, and with them all forms of sickness and trials.

Here in Exodus God gives us one of the most tremendous promises given in the Bible. He says He will take sickness away from the midst of you and the number of thy days will be fulfilled. How do you react to such a heady promise when we see all around us the very opposite. A world full of pain and suffering, with bodies decimated by disease and lives snuffed out prematurely. The medical profession gives us some glimmer of hope on this human battlefield but still the carnage is heavy and the numbers are not good. Greed has crept in to the medical community almost voiding out the hypocritical oath, television commercials trying to sell us every drug imaginable, planting thought seeds of sickness asking questions like "do you feel this way?" "Ask your doctor"? Sadly they are only selling band aides, and tonics, and never even address the core of the problem. Only when we address our Three Fold Nature, our special uniqueness, our comingling of humanity and deity do we feel the subtle essence of Spirit within. Ezekiel 36:26 a new heart (mind) I will give you and a new spirit will I put within you. It's not so much of a new spirit, as it is a glorious awakening of the spirit you already possess. It is a power that operates within you, a presence, inspiring, guiding, and sustaining you, and if we consciously attune ourselves to it, it will flow through your entire being transforming your spiritual, emotional, mental and physical side of life like nothing else can. It will more than address your three fold nature; it will restore the natural man and return you to a life of firing on all cylinders in no time. Remember you have a body, mind, and a soul.

You've Got That Right

Acts 19:11

And God wrought special miracles by the hands of Paul so that from his body were brought unto the sick handkerchiefs or aprons, and the diseases departed from them. Then certain of the vagabond Jews, exorcists, took upon themselves to call over them which had evil spirits the name of the Lord Jesus, saying we adjure you by Jesus who Paul preached and the evil spirits answered and said Jesus I know, and Paul I know but who are you? And the man in whom the evil spirit was leaped on them, and overcame them, and prevailed against them so that they fled out of that house naked and wounded and bleeding.

I would like to start off today by relaying to you a little episode that happened to me rather recently while I was working out. I work out mainly at home because of time constraints that don't allow me to get to the gym very often. I was in the middle of a set of sit ups when a friend of mine stopped by. With a coy little smile on his face he was laughing at me while I sweated up a storm. When I asked him what was so funny he told me he would be having a rock-hard abdomen and will lose 30 pounds in three weeks without lifting a finger or dieting. I said really? He said yes and whipped out a bottle of pills called Carbo-Blasters he bought off the T.V. (The ad snares people by telling them it's not for people with 15 to 20 pounds to lose but for those with a real weight problem). They can make these outrageous, totally false claims by adding a money back guarantee to the offer. The money back guarantee lets them off the hook, if it doesn't work for you and (99.9 percent of the time it won't) just send in for your refund. The manufacturer is counting on you not to go after them for a refund and less than 10 percent ever do. The manufacturer is trying to sell the motivation it takes, the sheer blood and guts and hard work that is required. That doesn't come in a bottle and those offers just never work. Ironically they tell you to take their super pills or concoctions in conjunction with a healthy diet and exercise. Duh! That is all you really need and it can never be put in a bottle or purchased with money. Good health is as free as sunshine.

Now I wasn't going to be the one to burst my buddies bubble but I knew that those pills weren't going to do anything for him. His whole life he had been a couch potato eating whatever he pleased and never exercising. I on the other hand had been the opposite. I played sports at a division 1A school Holy Name football, baseball and basketball. I took jeet kune do for a good portion of my youth and was a karate instructor for a number of years. I knew from experience that those pills were a rip-off and that my friend had been taken. But how did I know. I knew because over the years of both exercise and diet I had developed a Health Consciousness, it was a part of my life and that I had both experience and knowledge in the field. I had taken the time and effort to build a compartment in my mind, a slice of my life dedicated to the pursuing of health and all its components. It gave me a right to say: I know what I'm talking about. I couldn't be taken in by that ad but knew many people could be because they themselves never developed a Health consciousness, they never went through the pain and sacrifice to develop one and now they wanted to buy one in a bottle for only 179.95. It doesn't work that way with anything in life. What my friend was trying to do was purchase something he had no right of consciousness for, and me having those things saw his folly.

I see something very similar going on with a large segment of our culture today Christians included. They don't have a spiritual consciousness, they don't have a right to claim that they know what they're talking about. Their idea of God or their relationship with Him is vague, cloudy or weak at best. Then when faced with a tragedy or loss can't take full advantage of the graces of God, of His miracles and His healings. What does a miracle mean? It means that having called upon God things will be different from what they would have been had we not done so. They can be big, they can be small, but they are out there for us.

Often times a person feels abandoned by God and gives up on a relationship altogether. They feel they don't hear from Him, they don't see Him working in their lives. There is no connection. Listen there should be nothing more important to you than your pursuit of the Almighty in your life. The fruits of the spirit once attained are worth a king's ransom, totally priceless. What would you pay cash money for pure peace of mind and harmony in your life? How about some happiness, the thing everyone is trying to buy or steal or work for is amply available, throw a little health in there, not just physical but mental and what we have here is something very much worth pursuing and very attainable, priceless if you will. Many of us pursue the fountain of youth thru diet and exercise and that's all well and good, but God is the fountain of life, and the fountain of life sends forth living waters that awaken every faculty of mind and body, the more deeply we drink, the more spiritual or (in tune with God) we become. Jesus said, "I am the bread of life, I am the door of life, I am the way of life, my words are Spirit and they are life". Every affirmation of life adds new life. Press in close, learn to lean on God and develop yourself a consciousness for Him as you would with health or music or business, for He came that we may have life and have it more abundantly.

What is a consciousness for something? It is a space or compartment, an area of your life and mind given over to the pursuit of that subject. Be it music, money, or God. To try to attain something without having the consciousness for it is a form of stealing and Moses says "Thou shall not steal" in essence you really can't steal what you don't have a mind for, you can try and try but you won't succeed. To be successful in any field of endeavor you must have the consciousness that corresponds to it. To be healthy, you must have a health consciousness, prosperous a prosperity consciousness; you must have what it takes. We cannot keep anything we do not have the mind for and "thou shall not steal" reverberates that ideal. Moses is not pleading with us not to steal; he is saying we can't steal even if we want to. God's law meters out perfect justice. It may seem to someone as if they had gotten away with something, but the wheels of life grind slowly and that person will never be able to retain what was not theirs to begin with. When God says "Thou shall not steal" He means it. You must develop within yourself the consciousness that corresponds to your goals. If it is health, you need a health consciousness, if it is God you seek, a spiritual consciousness, money a prosperity or money consciousness. Then no man may break in and steal it from you, it is yours for all time.

This account from Acts at the top of the page hits the nail on the head as far as this teaching is concerned. Paul having one of the greatest spiritual consciousness's to ever grace this planet could heal people without even being there. Similar to the sick woman that reached out in faith to touch Jesus's garment and was healed immediately, Paul was able to do much the same thing.

Impressed with the power Paul possessed a group of vagabond Jews tried to copy him and cast out demons invoking Jesus's name. But they did not have the necessary groundwork needed in their minds, hearts, or consciousness's. They had not built up a proper relationship with the Lord that Paul had and were exposed as frauds. Jesus I know, Paul I know, but who are you asked the demon? It can be quite dangerous to do this in our own lives, that evil spirit or that bad situation, leaped upon them, when it leaps upon you, will you know what to do? Will you have to run away naked, beaten and screaming.

When life problems creep in and leap upon you, will you be victorious or run away naked, wounded and bleeding? Will you call on the name of Jesus and not be heard? Build up within yourself a strong appetite for God, seek Him, press in and get to know Him and have the power within you to obtain victory in all the situations in your life. Never run away naked and wounded again, but boldly proclaim His presence, and humbly accept His authority in your life, for now you have that right.

Dominion

Listen people, make no mistake about this. We were not made to be put on this earth to be kicked around like a bunch of rag dolls, to be pushed to and fro by the worries of life with no control. Actually it is quite the contrary. In Genesis 1:28 God gives us the very first command, the very first inclining of what's expected of man, "Be fruitful and multiply, replenish the earth and subdue it and to have dominion over every living thing". He plainly wants us to subdue our environments and have dominion.

I would like to share with you one man's definition of Dominion from a very unlikely source, but never the less the truth. Opening scene of the movie The Departed, Jack Nicolson playing mobster Whitey Bulger says-"Ya know-I really don't want people to think that I'm a product of my environment, but rather that my environment is a product of me". Considering the source no truer words have ever been spoken.

We are not meant to be products of our environments. We are commanded to subdue our environments and by the power of the Holy Spirit, Christ's very nature inside of us, we are to make our environment products of us. We are not children of happenstance, bad luck or lousy circumstances as many believe but we have been given the power of Dominion through the gift of the Holy Spirit to change the unwanted or negative condition in our lives. Never believe it is the will of God for us to suffer. God will allow suffering and affliction to get our attention in an area of our lives, as lessons. Just how temporary that lesson is up to us, he gives us all the tools we need to overcome it and learn by it. We don't need resignation to lousy situations in our lives, we need resolution over them.

What good is it if Jesus's victory over sin gets us into heaven, yet our lives down here get decimated and destroyed by that very same sin we are forgiven of. There's a conundrum if I ever heard one. Jesus's salvation is for both heaven and earth. We are not to allow the negative things in life to leap upon us, overcome us, and make us flee naked, wounded and bleeding. Our environments, our lives should reflect and be by products of our indwelling spirit. Peace, Joy, Love and Abundance. This leads me to a missing ingredient in many a sincere Christians lives. This missing ingredient when added to the recipe of a Christian life will make all the difference in the world.

Passion

Passion and Dominion are ever linked. Without passion for music I would never have spent the time and effort it took to acquire an amount of expertise on the guitar. Which opened up a wonderful world of self-expression and worship through the magical outlet of music? Without passion someone like Michael Jordan would never have dominated the sport of basketball like he did. It was passion that brought Leonardo's artwork to life and made page after page fall from the desk of William Shakespeare. Without a certain amount of passion for the Lord and His word; you will never reach the heights He has planned for your life. That is because you will not seek after Him enough, you will not seek after Him with any kind of real passion or excitement. He is always peripheral and incidental.

Lack of passion will lead someone to say, God feels distant, He doesn't hear me and I don't really hear from Him, He doesn't seem very real in my life. I go through the religious motions but it doesn't translate very well into my everyday life. Listen and understand this, we don't serve a distant God or a moody God or temperamental God. Our God does not play favorites either. The only ones that are moody, distant and temperamental are ourselves and you can be assured of that.

And as far as favorites are concerned, whenever I say God doesn't play favorites inevitably someone will come up to me and say wasn't David one of Gods' favorites, or Moses ? I say no. David wasn't God's favorite, God was David's favorite. God was David's passion and that's what allowed him to live such a glorious and passion filled life. As flawed as David was and he was flawed as we all are, he was still a tremendous man of God.

People get scared when you say you must have passion for the Lord. They picture Trappist monks chanting on for hours in their hillside retreat. God desires for us to have passion for everything passion for your kids, wife, passion for your business, your job, the Red Sox, the Patriots, all areas of your life. In the Psalms we are told to, "Delight thyself also in the Lord and He will give you the desires of your heart". This is a command to delight thyself in life, to have fun, to have passion but to also have that same passion and fun towards the Lord and He will give you everything money can't buy and then some. Delight thyself also in the Lord, key word being also. Give Him space in your life, (consciousness).Make the time for talking to Him and make prayer and meditation the cornerstone of your life. Have passion for Him, and He will have passion for you. You will hear from Him, you will perceive his presence more deeply. You will learn to trust and the rest will take care of itself.

Listen, where your passion is, is where your heart is at. Your passion can be used as a gauge to see the level of your relationship with God. For years I loved competition, sports, music and the Lord. Those are my passions. In my late teens to early twenties music dominated my life. I didn't have much time for anything else, doing shows, travel, and practice took up all my energies and focus. You didn't see me much at church.

In my twenties and thirties softball and basketball gobbled up a good amount of my energies and focus. The best leagues always played on Sunday mornings hence forth you still didn't see me much in Church or in the Word. Then after years of nibbling and tasting Gods' word, accumulating in me, the passion scales tipped and more and more of my focus went into my relationship with God. Nothing has been the same since. I still love music; still love sports, thank God for my wife Nancy who loves sports also or we would both be in trouble. Always remember your Christian walk is a process. But when those passion scales tipped toward God the most, I started to receive in my life the desires of my heart, things money can't buy, health, joy and peace. Then there's no going back. The infinite richness of God is mine to enjoy. Vital good health, unspeakable joy, wisdom, all mine. There is a fullness within me keeps me ever satisfied and surely goodness and mercy shall follow me all the days of my life.

What was Jesus's passion? It's still the same thing it was two thousand years ago, healing. When Jesus physically walked this earth who can deny that His passion was healing. It still is today. Can you imagine the satisfaction and joy He got out of healing someone? Jesus passion for healing is still alive and well today as it ever was.

Healing in many ways comes naturally to the body. When you cut your arm what do you do/ nothing. Cover it up, forget about it. We don't linger our minds on such trivial things. We know it will heal. Given time a scab comes, a scab goes, it's good as new. All the while you are totally unaware of this little miracle taking place naturally.

When we deal with thoughts like depression, fear, anger and unforgiveness these are like cuts on the soul, and these things we do linger our minds on to our own detriment, but they can heal pretty much the same way as a cut on a finger. Naturally without any effort on our part by walking in the Spirit. Acknowledge Him and all things and He will make clear your path. Believe in your hearts of hearts that it is Gods' great pleasure to give us the keys to the kingdom and to bless us. We don't beg God to heal us, we just realize the truth, really realize the truth. It is Jesus's passion yesterday and today to wipe the pain from your face and replace it with joy. Listen when he tells you to go on and suffer no more. Turn your face to the Son and the shadows shall fall behind you. Turn your mind to the Lord and you will never run away, bloodied and beaten again.

Matthew 22:37-40 Jesus said unto him "thou shalt love the Lord thy God with all thy heart, with all thy soul and with thy entire mind. And thou shall love thy neighbor as thy self, that is loving passionately.

Heart Of The Matter

In Matthew chapter 22 Jesus is being tested by the Pharisees. They want to entangle Him in His words, snare Him in blasphemy. They ask Him His views on taxes, marriage rights in heaven, and which is the greatest of all Commandments. His answers did what truth and wisdom always do for they were astonished and marveled at His doctrine. This piece of scripture is so incredibly powerful, not because of eloquence or wit, but because it was simply the piercing truth, the unmistakable wisdom of God pouring forth and when it was done Matthew 22:46 says no man was able to answer Him a word. Out of the multitudes not a single heckler, no one would speak neither dared any man ask Him anymore misleading or self-incriminating questions. He tamed the doubting multitudes with an honest heart, the word of God, and the seeds of divine Love. He did it sublimely, with quiet confidence and assurance that only speaking the truth can give you. He goes on to give us one of those earth shaking statements that many people seem to miss completely or gloss over entirely. In Matthew 22-40 Jesus says that He can condense the entire Bible, all of the Prophets, all of Gods laws into just two commandments. Two commandments, centuries of God inspired wisdom, all the teachings of Moses, Abraham, and David condensed into two commandments. We all know Jesus was concise but this is taking brevity to a whole new level. Using wisdom and patience to chip away at all the unnecessary accretions Jesus was well aware of the layers and layers of religiosity weighing down Gods people, and miss-spent tradition watering down Gods word. In Jesus' day just as today, there were many divisions many opinions and many different denominations sparring with each other over who holds unto to Truth. Jesus like a master sculptor, a true Michelangelo, used the chisel of wisdom and the hammer of patience to chip away at all the unnecessary stratum to reveal that which is spotless, undying, and eternal. Matthew 22:40 Jesus said that on these two commandments we can hang all the laws and prophets. All the laws and prophets, when Jesus makes a statement of this magnitude, such as this, we better listen for He is peeling back all the layers, all the disguises, all the distortions to get to the true heart of the matter. The culmination of it all is that there is no force on this planet, no force in this universe greater than Divine Selfless Love. It is not mere emotion or sappy sentiment it is a pure state of knowledge, which lifts the soul above the dominion of this world and into a victorious revelation of the supremacy of an all loving God.

When Jesus compressed and filtered all of Gods' laws, all His prophets all His teachings, all of what He really is into two simple commandments, two simple statements, He at that moment was looking into the incredible potential that the human heart (mind) possesses. He knew that buried beneath the immense mass of rules and regulations, tradition and miss-spent beliefs was the only thing that truly mattered, the only thing of true and eternal worth. He knew hidden deep within the recesses of every human heart was the Spirit of Divine Love, seeds of selfless love. All else, everything will perish, except that flame that spark of truth, that is immortal and perfect. Jesus was able to love unconditionally, to guide us, teach us and heal us, regardless of how He was treated because when He looked at us He saw past all of the limitations and ridiculousness of human reasoning to see the thing that is perfect, that is priceless. That spirit of Divine Love. It is this spirit of Divine Love that makes us into His image and likeness, and when all is stripped away it is this spirit of love that continues on. It is toward the complete realization of this Divine Love that the whole of the world is moving, not just this world but the entire universe in general. It is for this purpose, that we were separated unto Him, chosen, but the world does not see it this way. At its present level of understanding humanity continues to grasp at fleeting shadows, and shards of happiness, ignoring in our blindness the true substance, the all in all of Divine Love. So suffering and sorrow continues on until the world learns from its self-inflicted pain. The world does not yet at its present stage of evolution understand and comprehend a love that is selfless, pure and divine. The type of love that Christ possessed is very much foreign to us. We are engrossed in the pursuit of our own pleasures. We have little interest for the real and abiding things of life.

So Jesus in an effort to make it as simple as possible stripped it all down to its absolute core it's very essence. Residing deep within each of us hidden under the many layers of misconception and blindness is the seed of Divine love. Divine love distinguishes itself from human love in many ways. Human love is exclusionary and fickle. Divine love is free from all partiality and prejudice. Divine love embraces the whole universe it is pure, and it seeks nothing for itself. It resides only in the heart that has ceased from all judgment and condemnation and that heart once having glimpsed the incomprehensible magnificence, the glorious beauty of such a love, will never again rest in its selfishness and weakness, but will pursue that love, fervently and with tenacity until it is beating in perfect harmony with it. This is spiritual power. It is a force to be reckoned with and it was the power Jesus was speaking of earlier in Matthew 22:29 when He said ye err not knowing the scriptures nor the power of God.

How can I love the violent? The liar, the thief, there is only one way, when we love in selfless love, divine love. It opens our eyes to compassion and compassion lends itself to understanding. We can then perceive the tragic path by which these people have become as they are, we can feel their intense suffering and pain. A heart filled with divine, selfless love no longer has room in it for condemnation and judgment. We are enlightened to the fact that the world does not yet understand a love that is totally selfless. Jesus was most misunderstood because of the purity of His love and motives. He wasn't driven by the pursuit of His own fleshly pleasures, or ambitions, he wasn't ceaselessly trying to establish the next big mega church. He was driven by a Divine Love, a love that is purer than gold and priceless in value. Jesus having both patience and compassion for the Pharisees, the very ones trying to undermine and bring Him down, told them the two secrets of a victorious life. If you knew someone was trying to trip you up, hurt you in some form or fashion would you dispense to them heartfelt advice and guidance or would you snub your nose at them, wouldn't your defenses go up and wouldn't you scratch them off the proverbial Christmas list and prepare for a fight. Jesus displaying selfless Divine Love without skipping a beat said to them Matthew 22:37 "Thou shalt love the Lord thy God, with all thy heart, and with all thy soul, and with thy entire mind". This is the first and greatest commandment. God comes first, you can't, your family cant, He has to. All else will fall into place if you put what belongs first, first. Jesus knew this. When Jesus says love thee with all thy heart He is speaking of the emotional charge the mind gives for something. Love is the emotional investment of the mind. It is something you must give out consciously and freely not some involuntary or natural reaction. We know Biblically speaking that the heart is a metaphor for the mind. We know love is an emotional response of the mind, not the fleshy organ pumping blood throughout your body. Yes it is much more poetic and romantic to say I love you with all my heart then to say I love you with my entire mind but make no mistake about it they are one in the same.

Matthew 22:37 Thou shall love the Lord thy God with all thy heart and with all thy soul and with thy entire mind.

Jesus includes both so we have no confusion. He throws the soul in these also to incorporate the entire being. He alludes to the symbiotic existence of the entire being leaving out nothing. Jesus undoubtedly fired on all cylinders and then some. We must love and seek God first above everything and give Him our entire being and then it shall be added unto you. There is no half-hearted or halfway when it comes to God. He demands our best. In Exodus Gods first commandment to Moses was "Thou shalt have no other gods before me" and Jesus is just reiterating this eternal message". We must love God with all our bodies, minds and souls. He wants all of us, and by doing so we receive within ourselves a love so pure, so powerful, it reaches to the heavens and stretches to the sky. To center one's life on these two great laws of love is to enter into rest, peace and harmony. Until this great principle is realized the soul is not established in peace and understanding and we cannot live within the simplicity of an honest heart. Where you find endless patience, lowliness, self-control, gentleness, and enduring sympathy you find Divine Love. Seek the company of such people for they live with the eternal, they understand, they have goodwill toward all creatures, irrespective of race, color or creed. They know that the Divine Spark within them is no different than the Divine Spark that is encompassed within others. They see God in everyone they meet, there are no strangers no aliens.

Sometimes in life God guides us with the deftness of a feather stroke and other times when we refuse to "see things correctly" He will use something a little more poignant, a little more direct, like a sledge hammer. It was a sledge hammer I needed to free me from the ice like grip of unforgiveness that had invaded and stagnated my heart. Some years ago I went through a nightmare time in my life. I was married, I had 3 children and all-consuming job with a hefty mortgage to boot. Sound familiar. Making ends meet was sometimes a struggle but we got by. Than one day almost out of the blue, my wife informed me she wants out. No real reasonable explanation, she just wanted out. To me it seemed as if she had just flipped a switch inside herself and turned off her love toward me. No one is perfect inside any relationship but this was too much. I spent years in a demanding job to provide, felt I had truly done everything possible to "do the right thing" yet in the end there was no changing her mind. I was completely and totally devastated and confused. Angry didn't even begin to define how I felt. There was nothing I could do and we were divorced a year later. In all fairness I understand that there are always two sides to a story but you're going to have to read her book to get her side so for right now suffice it to say you're stuck with just mine. Years went by and time heals so they say or so I thought. Truth is time doesn't heal it only buries things, only by the grace of God do we truly heal. We had children together so we still had to deal with each other from time to time, holidays, etc. Years went by and I met a wonderful, pure hearted woman named Nancy and started rebuilding my life, but something inside still nagged at me. My ex and I were very civil to one another and on a human scale of things I thought I had forgiven her. But deep down deep within me I hadn't, for whenever I would hear of misfortune that would come her way I would secretly rejoice. Phrases like, good she got what she deserves, or see what goes around comes around would bring me a sick satisfaction that proved my forgiveness was counterfeit. Little did I realize that this "sore of unforgiveness" on my heart was affecting my everyday life adversely, subtly stealing joy and love from my new life, my new beginning and invading my dreams and decisions. We mire ourselves (as humans) in unfathomable complexities when the truth is pure simplicity. I was clinging so subtly to my self-imposed anger. It took the sledge hammer of truth to knock me off my perch and awaken me from my slumber. You can hear Gods voice in the rustle of the leaves, you hear it in the crashing of a wave, in the screech of an eagle, in the crying of an infant, or on the lips of a song. Always cock your head and listen for the myriad of ways the Lord will reach out to you in your time of need or growth. It was exactly that on the lips of a song that God, infinite in His wisdom knew I was ready to hear. God will use any and all means to reach us. He will breakdown all barriers and fortresses to get at that all important Heart of the Matter.

It was a beautiful spring day, and we were finishing off the final preparations for our first "Seeker Service" that we were hosting in a new church plant called Blackstone Valley Community Church. The pastors wife Debbie asked me if I would perform a special number during the service, it was an unusual choice of music for a church service but being a seeker service we allowed for it. It was a song by Don Henley and it was called, Heart of the Matter. Years earlier it was a huge hit off his solo debut so I had some familiarity with it. But as I learned the music to it and as I was memorizing the lyrics something profound was happening to me. The Lord was forcing me to face the facts, through this song, He was making me realize deep down, and at the very heart of the matter I'd never really forgiven Sandy. We were hospitable and civil toward one another but there was always a subtle underlying current of hurt, pain and remorse. I'm sure many a divorced couple feels this way, but the problem with it is until you have gotten over it, until there is true and honest forgiveness, a closure, you carry the unwanted baggage and negatively charged emotions forward with you into all your new relationships and situations. These hurtful emotions will continue to mar and stain all your future plans, many times without you even realizing what is going on. Forgiveness allows you to go on cleanly minus the baggage, to begin anew, free and clear.

Don Henley is not a preacher, pastor, or prophet he is a musician and a human being. He's a human being who has shown through music that he really gets it when it comes to forgiveness of someone that has hurt you. He gets it. He truly understands that there are people in your life, who've come and gone, they let you down, hurt your pride, but you better put it all behind you because life goes on. You keep carrying that anger it'll eat you up inside, I've been trying to get down to the heart of the matter, because the flesh will get weak and your thoughts will scatter, but I think it's about forgiveness. Forgiveness even if you don't love me anymore. The music accompanying these pearls of wisdom is perfect, the feel is perfect and the message is perfect. It conveys honest forgiveness in a way that only music could do. If you get a chance listen to the song over again so you know where I'm coming from. As I stepped out on that stage that Sunday morning I was in for a major surprise. I had no idea that my son had invited Sandy to the service. He was participating in a drama skit and thought she might want to see him in it. That's all fine and dandy but he failed to tell me. So there she sat with her new husband Tony, The words and music to the song had awakened my soul and softened my heart and 'though there were quite a few people there in attendance that morning I sang that song exclusively to her. No one else in that service knew what was happening except me and Sandy. I barley was able to get the words out, but we both knew a miracle was taking place. In the midst of that song, I let go of all the anger, all the hurt, all the pain, everything that was holding me back from my new life. It all just emptied out of me like the air from a balloon and I knew at that very instant that all that the Lord was trying to teach me about the Power of forgiveness was at hand.

Forgiveness isn't for the person you're forgiving it is for you. I understand that now. Forgiveness is a gift to those who love the Lord thy God with all their heart, with all thy soul and with their entire mind, as Jesus commanded. This selfless Divine Love allows us compassion, compassion to understand another individual and not just to judge them. It allows us to enter into their intense suffering with understanding. Immersed in supreme love we seek not to condemn, not to brand or classify for we are not judge and jury, for there is only one whose heart is pure enough to judge. To realize Divine Love lifts the soul to that point of pure vision where love, goodness and justice are all conquering and indestructible. It then allows us to go forth and fulfill Jesus' second great commandment to love our neighbor as ourselves. Listen stop being swayed and dominated by the old elements of self, be reborn and empty thyself and let God fill you with that pure selfless love that divine power that He speaks of in Matthew 22:37. The ability to truly forgive is the ultimate expression of Divine Love, it is a healer that has no past, and lives and breathes only in the moment. It leaves all judging to God and it flourishes everywhere it goes. It is what made Jesus the true Son of God and it is what we all must cultivate if we are to proceed any further in life. Do not err, know your scriptures and feel the power of God. Let the higher form of love dominate you and you will be firing on all cylinders.

Righteous Anger

There is no such thing as righteous anger toward another human being. There is no hatred no matter how justified that is allowable before God. Jesus nullified all that with the greatest display of selflessness the world has ever witnessed. His actions on the cross leave us in stunned silence. Jesus poured out forgiveness to the very people that were killing Him, as they were killing Him. Think about that. He didn't take a time out to think things over, He didn't let a few years go by to soften the memory or let time heal He did it while they were in the very act. He turned the other cheek while the blood was still warm and flowing. In the midst of the pain, in the midst of the agony, in the midst of all that suffering, He displays a Divine Love we can only at the moment aspire to. In return He saved the world from itself with forgiveness as its cornerstone. When the heavy Roman mallet fell and the six inch nails pierced his hands He winced "Father forgive them". When the blood from the crown of thorns would sting His eyes He whispered, "Father forgive them". When the heavy blood soaked cross was lifted up, and the wrenching pain of all His weight was too much to bear He cried out, "Father forgive them for they know not what they do". Now let's pause for one second, let's contemplate just what He did. All the pain, all the suffering, being in the very moment he forgave them. Now what was it that your brother did to you? What was it that your sister said? Does it stack up against what was done to our Lord and Savior? I think not. If you snub your nose at this teaching, this example, this eternal law, no matter how justified you feel, you and no one else is making a conscious decision not to partake in the "Power of God" that is forgiveness. Jesus said, "You err, not knowing the scriptures or the Power of God". This clinging to what we sometimes feel is justified anger is the root of all evil. It is the birth of much of the sickness and disease this world must bear. Its ugly scar has plagued this planet ever since we appeared on the scene and until we get some semblance of Divine Love in our lives it will remain, tarnishing all it comes in contact with.

Wars which devastate and destroy entire nations are by products of unforgiveness and righteous anger. Families that are torn apart never to reunite again stand steadfast in their stubbornness and unforgiveness. Individuals whom compromise their souls and all its potential for good, only to cling ferociously to the anger and hurt that binds and sickens them, do it because they feel they have the right that no one can do that to me and get away with it. This misconception only lengthens their sentence of self-imposed pain, anger and sickness for make no mistake about it to harbor these powerfully negative emotions only brings harm both physically and mentally to the body. Holding on to anger and even taking it the step further, wanting revenge, is you consciously rejecting the Highest teaching, the most important lesson our Lord has for us. Look at the price He had to pay to deliver it. His uttering of those words, "Father forgive them for they know not what they are doing" proves to me unequivocally that Jesus Christ was the true Son of God. We all want to be forgiven, we all want to be whole, we all want God's blessing and favor in our lives but we ourselves will not be forgiven, we will not be able to partake in the richness that is life until we become ourselves ambassadors for forgiveness, Mark 11:25-26 states in Jesus's own words, "and when you stand praying forgive, if you have anything against anyone so that your Father in heaven may forgive you of all your trespasses. He continues on with a stern warning saying," if you don't forgive neither will your Father which is in heaven forgive you". Are you hearing that are those words seeping in? Do you now realize the importance of your forgiving? Your entire spiritual life depends upon it, and there is no moving forward there is no ascending of the heights without it. To love God with all your heart, mind and soul is to be pointed toward forgiveness. It fulfills Gods greatest commandment Matthew 22:37, also allowing you the ability to fulfill the second greatest commandment, "love your neighbor as yourself" and to know the Power of God. As we strive each day, we detach ourselves more and more from the inward selfishness we call unforgiveness. When we temper our emotions, when we calm our powerful personalities and diminish our unwanted lusts we will know that the Divine is awakening within and that you are drawing nearer to that eternal flame, the very fire of life that is Selfless love. All of life is predicated on these two commandments and these two commandments are predicated on the all suffering power of love. We forfeit our rights as Christians when we coddle hurt, and anger, and unforgiveness within ourselves. Our relationship toward God becomes tainted, stained and weakened and God tells us straight up in Matthew 5:23-24 not to even come to God until you have dealt with this destructive emotion, the barrier of all barriers. Jesus says and I quote "Therefore if thou shall bring thy gift to the alter and there remembers that thy brother has aught "an issue" against thee, listen now leave thy gift before the alter and go thy way, first be reconciled to thy brother or sister and then come and offer thy gift. Regard your failings, your shortcomings, your sufferings, as Gods voice telling you clearly where you are weak and faulty. Every whiff of pain will show you exactly where you need work and what needs to be remedied in order to bring you closer to all its glorious beauty. We all must work with great persistence, and diligence, and cease to be swayed and dominated by the old elements of self. We must be reborn into the true realization of Divine Love. When the human heart and mind are emptied of self then the love that is of God will enter and dominate.

This love flowing through you will harmonize everything in your experience, it will bring joy and gladness, it will leave with you an immutable sense of security, as we learn to love the many equally as we do the few. Pierre Diehard De Chardin once wrote; "Someday, after we have mastered the winds, the waves, the tides and gravity, we shall harness . . . the energies of love. Then for the second time in human history, we will have discovered fire".

Hate and anger are a boomerang, throw it at somebody and it will come back to hit you. Forgiveness is an antidote for poisons such as hatred and anger that lie smoldering and seething inside just waiting to be fanned into an all-consuming flame. Leaning on the verse, "Vengeance is mine" sayeth the Lord, "I will repay", alleviates all need for revenge, the Lord will not stand up for us if we insist upon lashing out and taking things into our own hands. In that case we are on our own without the Lords blessing, further more whatever action that is taken on your part will have to be recompensed again (we reap what we sow) so you are only truly hurting yourself when you set out to hurt another. Listen any negative action taken by you no matter how justified you feel will bring negative circumstances right back to you, grain for grain, measure for measure, make no mistake about it. These are universal laws laid down by God. Work with them not against them. Jesus was a healer and His gift of forgiveness is a healer also. It will not only heal your body of the ailments associated with hurt and disappointment it can reach right into all the elements of your life and heal them to. It can heal your family, it can heal your job, and it can even heal your environment.

Two years before my divorce we had moved into a first floor apartment in the city. After the divorce I remained there and my ex moved out. It was a nice apartment and a nice location, but I had so many negative memories and emotions linked to the residence that I absolutely hated the place. I mean I HATED the place, just in case I didn't get that across plainly enough. Even though I hated the place, affordable apartments were hard to come by so I continued to live there out of necessity. Just in case I didn't make myself plain, I hated the kitchen, I hated the bathroom, I hated the bedroom, I even hated the depressing wallpaper I had to stare at every morning while I had my tea and read my paper. If I could have afforded to move it would have been "exit stage left" a long time ago. That not being the case I settled in and made the best for I really had no other choice. When I finally gave in to the Healing Power of Forgiveness, when I chose to stop the anger and hurt, when I truly realized there is a way to overcome every situation thru the use of a power greater than me, life began again. Life for me was renewed, I was finally moving forward once more. Ezekiel 36; 26 "A new heart will I give you, and a new spirit will I put within you". That scripture will forever ring true for me and I quote it to this day with the same authority as the original writer.

Revelation 21: 7 "He that overcomes shall inherit all things and I will be his God and he shall be my son". I overcame the subtle sickness of unforgiving. I came out of the enveloping darkness and into a newer brighter life. It changed everything. The apartment I hated so much, that place I despised so intensely, I wound up buying the building a little more than a year later. We renovated from top to bottom making the place modern, beautiful and bright and all the decrepit feelings I had toward the place went right in the dumpster, along with the horse hair plaster and old ceiling tiles. It is hard for me to believe that I can sit here while writing this book and say with all honesty that I love this place. I scarcely believe it myself but it's true. Forgiveness healed my body, forgiveness healed my soul and forgiveness healed my home, and Forgiveness will heal you!!!

Revelations 21:7 "He that overcometh shall inherit all things, I will be his God and he shall be my son". So let see what our choices are. We can grip the icy hand of unforgiveness or believing in Gods words we can overcome all things, be a son or daughter of God, and Fire on All Cylinders Forever.

Your mind is your gateway to your soul, without the level of intelligence are minds create we could never have a meaningful, back and forth relationship with God for God is the perfect balance of love and intelligence. Our minds and our thinking govern every aspect big and small in our lives. Jesus revolutionized mankind's relationship to God. He revealed it to be both personal and parental. His teachings and the subsequent New Testament are a metaphysical and psychological treasure trove unmatched and unequalled anywhere. His total understanding of the human psyche is revealed to us within its pages. Whether it is a lesson in life to be taken literally, or a timeless parable open to all, his words are living and breathing "signposts of life" giving us direction and guidance whenever we may need it. But the sad fact is many a person's Bible does nothing but collects dust or takes up shelf space in most people's homes. "We ERR not knowing the scriptures or the Power of God". Those aren't my words but they are from the mouth of Jesus Himself, spoke nearly two thousand years ago but more relevant today than ever. His words live and breathe and His very being is found within them. Are we so powerful so self-absorbed that we fail to see the worth of these "words of life". I pray not, for once these pearls of wisdom are revealed to you, when their light shines within the dark recesses of your innermost being, there is no going back. Once in the arms of our Lord, human love like salt loses its flavor, and divine love and all its glory will be all that you seek. Once having tasted filet mignon, simple hamburger just will not do.

Viva Viagra

Pfizer, Glaxo Smith Kline, Roche, Eli Lilly these pharmaceutical giants, these behemoths of capitalism, would love you to believe that they are the "saviors" of the world. That they are the great healers of the day, Jesus in pill form. That they have an answer and a cure for all your ills and maladies. Some of their products again I say are quite miraculous and I thank God for their discovery. Remember this, they did not create these drugs, God revealed them, and I purchase them and use them when needed. Antibiotics alone have saved countless millions of lives, since its emergence on the scene. I have enormous respect for the medical community and all of its branches, but I do draw the line when it comes to "purposely manipulating" and mildly brainwashing the unsuspecting public into buying their products. The egregious proliferation of advertising spear headed by these pharmaceutical giants only proves beyond doubt, that they only want to raise your "consciousness, raise your awareness" of the disease and sickness that is seemingly all around you, to plant (seeds of sickness) in the garden of your mind. They sow subtle suggestions of illness while turning the soul of your thoughts from potentially positive to definitively negative. If this raising of the awareness were done out of true and real concern for the person or the patient that would be one thing, but the fact is, it is not. It is fueled by profits and bottom lines. Billions of dollars are at stake and as soon as you throw that kind of money in a situation it will inevitably warp it. Their ads are meant to (create patients not treat them). Now that's sick!!!

Money spent on the airways is to make shareholders happy not you healthy. It would seem on the surface of many of these ads, and we have all seen them haven't we, that it is comforting knowing we have help for this ailment and a pill for that one. These companies seem almost noble in offering us help in easing our pain and suffering, it's not noble it's infuriating. Watching T.V. the other night I counted 16 commercials related to one sickness or another in a two hour span. Sixteen. They are so blatantly putting "thoughts of sickness" in your mind their nobleness goes right out the window. Some people do suffer from these ailments but you can bet a whole lot more suffer from them now, than before these ads flooded the markets. They have gone out of their way, not to mention spend hundreds of millions of dollars to educate me about R.L.S. Restless leg syndrome, my legs hurt at night sometimes, maybe I have it. Erectile dysfunction we won't even go there. I.B.S. irritable bowel syndrome, well I can be a pain in the ass sometimes. No scratch that I want to take a sleep additive that helps me sleep, but gives me suicidal thoughts, headaches, dizziness, nausea' yes that sounds even better. Our level of consciousness about health issues is being raised not for our welfare but for our pocketbooks. Truth is they want you to try as many of their products as possible whether you need them or not. It's pure manipulation and it used to be done on the subconscious level. Not anymore, today main stream corporate advertising is right in our faces sandwiched somewhere in between reruns of Desperate Housewives and Monday Night Football.

Don't let the advertising powers dictate to you what to think about. You choose what you want to contemplate on. But if you don't consciously choose what you want, you will be unconsciously force fed by your flat screen. Every waking hour we are at work building our consciousness, this work is silent and overlooked by the bulk of humanity. Even so it is your most important activity in life. Minute by minute, hour by hour, we are building either for our good, or for our bad, for our health or for our detriment. The beliefs that we allow ourselves to embrace, we inevitably demonstrate. We are the gate keepers. We must be vigilant. Pharmaceutical Companies arrive at their medical solutions, their procurement of drugs, by mixing this compound with that compound, this element, with that element, and then by observing how it reacts to the body do they finally arrive at a conclusion. Is it beneficial is it harmful, do the side effects outweigh benefits? Some of these drugs and cures are quite miraculous and we've come a long way. God has blessed mankind with a most incredible intellect. With the mixing of this, and the adding of that, we've eradicated some diseases all together, some like diabetes we've learned to control, others such as cancer, they are still searching. Who would have thought with a little pinch of this, we could develop things so powerful as penicillin, or morphine. What powerful effects these medicines have on the human body. Now I ask you who would have thought that we have something very similar going on right within our very own heads, our very own bodies, it is designed to work for our good, dispensing just what we need exactly when we need it. But when it gets the wrong orders this little pharmaceutical company left unchecked works toward our determent and we never even know it. When we mix powerful negative emotions (potions) and feeling, deep within ourselves, we are concocting all sorts of trouble in many shapes and forms. This "cauldron of the mind" this mixing of this negative emotion, with that detrimental thought, producing (reactions) "pills" we've already swallowed and side effects we are not going to like. This little (chem-lab) left on its own with its oblivious employees, and 24 hour staff, can really wreak havoc on the human body. Really the biggest difference I see between pharmaceutical medicine and our own internal industry, is that pharmaceutical drugs you must ingest, you must put them in your body to make them work, where as our internal drug company, the reaction that they produce, must be removed from your body, they must be taken out. Let me ask you one question in regards to your own body, would you rather let things go on randomly with no one in control or would you like to step in and be the pharmacist. Jesus Christ's teachings on the subject along with Paul's subsequent New Testament revelations puts you squarely in the driver seat, or behind the drug store counter, whichever way you want to see it. Jesus teaches us how to manufacture wonderful beneficial compounds within our bodies using the same method that sometimes destroys us our little "cauldron of the mind". It can be used consciously in the positive sense rather than unconsciously in the negative.

Let's create something here, let's take one part unforgiveness then lets add one part despair, mix steadily for a few years, now it's time to include a few fresh ounces of anger and just a speck of "deep rooted envy", take it 3 times a day every day for the rest of your life and I think you can see the relevance that thoughts and feelings and emotions can have on your life. This is a true prescription for disaster and it comes with unlimited refills to boot. I think you can see where this is going. It's monumental, but the fact is you can have control you can be the bartender, the mixologist, the pharmacist. You can only drink the drink you mix yourself so make it a good one. Your thoughts and emotions are the ingredients, your choices do the stirring and your body is the cup. When we fill it with life giving thoughts and good productive emotions, then and only then does everything comes back to us, everything that makes life worthwhile and everything that flows from the inner realm of fathomless joy. I lift up my whole mind to the realization that the spirit of God is within me, that His presence will guide me if I so choose. So now I invite this presence the indwelling Christ within to direct my thoughts and acts and direct me into new ways of doing things, new ways of thinking. I invite and expect new circumstances and new situations to present them-selves and I expect this new spirit in me to succeed in and through all its endeavors. I walk now with absolute assurance that there is that within me that sees knows and understands this truth and that completely accepts it and earnestly tries to express it. My body is forever renewed by this Spirit, I am now made vigorous and whole, I possess the vitality of the infinite, and every breath I draw is a breath of perfection. Every thought I hold is vitalizing, rebuilding and renewing every cell of my body. I wait on that presence that makes all things possible and all things perfect.

If we really want dominion over our bodies and this world, if we really want to take command of this spiritual instrument we call ourselves than listen and take heed of these words of Paul that was expressing the "Christ mind' that He possessed. Philippians 3:21 "Who shall change our vile bodies, that it may be fashioned like unto his glorious body"? Jesus and you working in conjunction can do just that. Philippians 3:12 "Not as though I had already attained, either were already perfect but "I Follow After". All that God really asks of us is that of our own freewill, we diligently, genuinely and earnestly strive after Thee. This is all accomplished without having to become a overbearing religious nut. It all happens naturally and subtly within the normal rhythm of your life. Philippians 3:13 Brethren, I count not myself to have apprehended but this one thing I do, forgetting those things which are behind, and reaching forth unto those things which are before. Philippians 3:14 "I press toward the mark for the prize of the high calling of God in Christ Jesus". To follow after and press toward the mark, that is your only requirement. Press forward with all your heart and mind and hold in memory these words in Philippians 4:6 "Be anxious for nothing, but in everything by prayer and supplication, with thanksgiving let your request be made known to God. And the Peace of God which surpasses all understanding shall keep your hearts and minds through Christ Jesus". Place these words in your heart and Jesus Christ will guard them for you. Dwell on that thought for a moment. The God of this universe will be your sentry, your personal protection. Now here comes some of the best psychological advice money can't buy.

Place these thoughts in the "cauldron of your mind" and give them a stir and then watch what will happen in your life. Philippians 4:8 "Finally brethren whatsoever things are true, whatsoever things are honest, whatsoever things are just, whatsoever things are pure, whatsoever things are lovely, whatsoever things are of good report, if there be any virtue and if there be any praise, think on these things, and the God of peace shall be with you. Listen "as a man thinketh so he is", is one of the greatest truths we have. Let us become conscious masters of what we allow into our stream of thoughts. Let us cut down on all the pollutants and wastes we inadvertently let in. Let's stop these pharmaceutical giants from planting thoughts of sickness in our heads. When we see an ad corresponding to a particular part of the body such as bladder problems, or high blood pressure rather than contemplating if you might have it, take that moment and say no. Reject it and say my Lord and Creator made me perfect, my bladder is perfect and pristine and functions completely as it is supposed to. We must not be divided between believing and doubting, we must know. We must carefully guard the mental reactions and not allow subverting thoughts entrance. Seek always to keep your thoughts affirmative and constructive. Advertisers prey on weak minds, ones they can manipulate and control. Don't be that person, know that the Divine Presence in you governs all things and that presence governs you. Know that at all times you have a silent, invisible partner guiding your every step. Today whatsoever thoughts are true, honest, just, pure, and lovely, are of good report and have any virtue and praise these and only these will I contemplate. Ads selling sickness I will reject, preachers that preach a "resignation to suffering I will reject. Christ did not need to suffer He could have demonstrated above it all at any time, He chose to suffer and die to prove that we may have victory over these things also. He is the Savior. With the "Christ mind" placed in me I will never subjugate myself to anything lower than His ideals, His reality, and His wholeness. Let the rest of the world embrace the lies and half-truths, I will embrace the "mind of Christ" and rise above the limitations of this world, as He did. Philippians 2:5 "Let this mind be in you which was also in Christ Jesus, who being in the form of God though it not robbery to be equal with God. Here is a wonderful "analogy to suffering" I was taught as a youngster but never forgot. If an infant who has never been taught that suffering and pain and lack in one's life is a forgone conclusion, has a pin from its diaper sticking in its side, does it say to itself, well I can put up with the pain until my diaper is changed or does it let out a blood curdling scream demanding that something is done. That baby will stop life on a dime until his situation is rectified. Two in the morning or two in the afternoon, doesn't matter, he or she will be heard. Don't resign yourself to suffering, be like the infant that hasn't learned the confining ways of the world yet, instead resign yourself to victory you have in Jesus today. 1 Chronicles 28:9 "Serve Him with a perfect heart, and a willing mind for the Lord searches all hearts, and understands all the "imagination of the thoughts". If thou seek Him, He will be found of thee. Your issues big or small are dear to the heart of the Lord.

We should never submit or resign ourselves to suffering, yes we should pray and ask Gods strength in the midst of turmoil, in the midst of pain, but not just to deal with it, but to absolutely overcome it. Praying to God for strength is only half the equation, praying for dominion over the situation is the other half. Jesus had dominion over sin, sickness, and death. He overcame all things and it is He that is our ultimate example. No other. Teaching resignation to suffering is really doing humanity a disservice, its teaching only half the truth. It's putting limitations on what God can do.

On my son Corey's fifth birthday I brought him to Toys R Us and told him he could pick out any bike he wanted. He chose a Power Rangers bike with dual brakes and training wheels. I never saw him so excited. They didn't have any more in stock so they shipped us one from another store. When it arrived I was at work and when I returned home I found a demoralized child crying because as he put it it's broke, it's all in pieces. He had spent hours trying to put it together but of course at that age it was way too difficult for him. I calmed him down, and told him we would have it together in no time. It took a little patience, a little time, and to be truthful, a little help from the neighbor, but we did it and for the next couple months he drove that thing right into the ground. He loved it. What I am driving at, or should say riding at, is this what seemed so impossible, so tragic, and so monumentally difficult for my 5 year old son was a piece of cake to his father. (And his neighbor) What seemed so difficult for the child was nothing to the father, (and his neighbor). What seems so out of reach for you is really nothing to the Father, and this Father doesn't need His neighbor. Often times one of the main reasons why our prayers go unanswered is that with our reasoning minds, we simply limit the power of God. Divine wisdom has a solution to any problem, any dilemma we might find ourselves in. What may seem monumental to us, insurmountable in our eyes is easily solved by Him (infinite wisdom). Have confidence in the Lord, have faith that He can do anything for it is not you doing it, it is He. Isaiah 55:11" so shall my word be that goeth forth out of my mouth, it shall not return unto me void, but it shall accomplish that which I please and it shall prosper in the thing where to I send it".

Human misery is both rampant and the norm in civilization today. It doesn't have to be that way for you. Would Jesus, had you met Him on a dusty road just outside of Bethlehem healed you only half way, or instead of healing you just give you the strength to continue on suffering with no end in sight. (Of course not) He would beyond a shadow of a doubt make you whole, and leave you with the words "go now and suffer no more". "You err, not knowing the scriptures or the power of God". Preachers and teachers and people who know the scriptures, do you know the Power of God also? They go hand in hand, two peas in a pod. Pray to God for the strength to overcome and nothing less. Before Jesus is introduced on the scene, we as a people, as a race had fallen woefully short of the Glory of God. Jesus commands us in Matthew 5:48 to "Be ye therefore perfect, even as your Father which is in heaven is perfect". This hints at the evolution of mankind spiritually. It seems to say that man though not fully developed yet has the ability or the potential to become divinely perfect. This does not make us God only the highest form of human being we can possible be. Jesus would not have us waste time or energy on something that was impossible. I'm not saying we are anywhere near it. I'm saying it's in the realm of possibility. Being a follower of Christ does not mean we must have perfection of character or a perfect life. Not a single person could "fit that bill". What is required is a genuine, honest, striving toward that perfection. The key here is not to limit God and not to limit your-self as a child of God.

Lions And Tigers And Bears Oh My!

A few years back I attended a play that was sponsored by my son's high school theatre guild. We arrived early to get ourselves some good seats and wound up just a few rows back but off to the left side of the stage. Due to the angle of our seats we were able to see a lot of the craziness that goes on behind the scenes. The actors and actresses were fidgeting with their costumes, going over their lines and checking their makeup. They were all hyped up with anticipation at the raising of the curtain and the beginning of the show. Just before the start, I watched the director gather the first ensemble of performers that would be in the opening number. They were all over the place, nervous and unfocused. She sternly looked at them and said, okay it's time now to "get into character" and get ready, we are about to begin. It was as if she had passed a magic wand over them, all the fidgeting stopped, and all the unnecessary chatter ceased and a steely look came over their faces that wasn't there seconds ago. They were in character now and had transformed in an instant into the role that he or she was playing. It went from bedlam backstage to a laser beam focus, and you could tell these kids meant business. The curtain went up and a wonderful time was had by all. This "getting into character" this focusing of ourselves is a technique we can use too. When we read about other people's lives and experiences within the context of the Bible, we also need to "get in character" and become that person ourselves for the Bible is the book of every man. Each poem, each parable, each psalm, each historical reference is aimed directly at you, and within each of these contains a spiritual lesson to be learned by you. Be the Doubting Thomas and learn that Christ is real, be the Good Samaritan and learn that race or creed can't stop you in your attempt to help others, be Lazarus and raise yourself from the tomb of the spiritually dead. We are called to play many roles as we flip through the pages of our Bibles. It really doesn't matter that some of these stories are centuries old and seemingly far removed from today's high tech life. They are as relevant for us today as the day they were penned. Doesn't matter that the stories sometimes involve first century camel herders or pre A.D. tent makers, it can just as easily be today's computer programmers or a used car salesman. These lessons in life and the principles they possess transcend time like no other writings can. We simply need to recognize ourselves within the context of the writing "getting in character" and import its teaching into our lives. The Bible is not a collection of stories about other people and other places. It is a collection of stories about you and your soul in the here and now.

Like I said we are called to play many roles and many characters. Sometimes it's a farmer (sower of the seed) (the word) that learns to sow on fertile ground. Matthew 13:1-23, sometimes it's a fisherman (who becomes a fisher of men); sometimes it's a roman centurion (who has enough faith to know Gods power to heal). But the role I want us all to "get in character" with today is the part of a lowly shepherd. So grab that staff firmly, lift your head to the sun, and get a whiff of that sheep poop, so we can begin.

Shepherds are one of the most prominent professions found in the Bible. Abel was the very first shepherd. King David himself started out as a lowly shepherd even the great Moses was brought down to a lowly shepherd before God could use him fully. But Jesus Christ of course was the greatest shepherd of all, The Good Shepherd. Christ constantly referred to His followers as His flock, but how can that relate to me today? I can see a pastor or a priest being called to shepherd like position, maybe someone in upper management, or heading up a company, but what does this have to do with the everyday man on the street, just trying to make a living? What am I supposed to lead? What am I supposed to shepherd? Okay here's the twist. Are you listening? Okay your flock, or your sheep, are your thoughts. I'll say it again, your flock, or your sheep, are your thoughts. Here's a thought. Every action you do, every word you say, anything that comes out of you, is preceded by a thought. This is a mental universe, and nothing happens in the physical till it first births itself in thought. Your thoughts hold great sway in your life, whether you realized it or not. Most people have no idea the degree their everyday thinking has in forming their existence or circumstances. In this regard ignorance is not bliss it's suicidal. 2: Corinthians 10 "For though we walk in the flesh we do not war after the flesh. For the weapons of our warfare are not of this world. On the contrary, they have the divine power to the pulling down of strongholds". Strongholds in this respect mean deep rooted thoughts or habitual behavior directly contrary to Gods word. But now here's the section I want to focus on, Paul says the "casting down imaginations", (or in English), controlling sinful thought and every high thing that exalts itself against the knowledge of God. Here's the payoff pitch and bringing into captivity every thought (did you hear that every thought) to the obedience of Christ. That little line just signs you up for local 147 of the Shepherds Union.

Bringing into captivity every thought involves bringing our thoughts into alignment with the will of Christ. Here are 4 steps to help bring you thought life under the Lordship of Christ:

1. Be aware that God knows every thought and that nothing is hidden from Him. We will have to account to God for our thoughts and as well as our words and actions. Always remember there can be no words spoken or no action taken that does not start off as thought.
2. Be aware that the battlefield is your mind. Some thoughts originate within us, while others come directly from outside influence. We can sometimes simultaneously be fighting two enemies at the same time. Our own sinful nature and outside negative influences.
3. Be steadfast in focusing your mind on Godly things. For is says in Romans 8:6-7 "for the mind set on the spirit is life and peace". Psalms 1; tells us to fill our

minds with God's word, and with those things which are noble, excellent, and praiseworthy.
4. Be careful what you let your eyes see, and your ears hear. Refuse and I emphasize refuse to let your eyes be and instrument for lust. Or to set any worthless or evil thing before your eyes, whether it be books, magazines, pictures, movies, television, or in real life.

We must remember it's all in the mind. That is the battlefield, and until we obtain some reasonable control over our thoughts God can't use us fully. It is a simple as that. God doesn't want us to be tossed to and fro by every wind of doctrine, but to display or demonstrate sound mind. We are not given a spirit of fear but of sound mind. I repeat until we demonstrate reasonable control over our thoughts or (being a good shepherd) God can't use you fully. Look at Moses God all along wanted to use Moses to free his people. It seemed to be all set up perfect, Moses was living in Egypt, in a position of power and influence, highly educated, but most of all he was considered kindred to the Pharaoh. He had the pharaoh's ear anytime he wanted it, perfect right. Wrong! Because Moses at that point in his life didn't have all his thoughts and emotions lined up just right yet. His sheep were running wild. Moses was very prone to anger. This loose emotion or lost sheep would cause him a lot of trouble. It would lead him to murder a man in a fit of rage, and hide his body in the sand. The great Moses wasn't ready yet to lead. The great Moses wasn't in control of his thoughts and emotions, and even though he was right where he was supposed to be (Egypt), God couldn't use him.

God had to take him totally out of his element. God changed his life completely, bringing him to a point where God could use him. Where was that point? Moses went from the Pharaohs court to a shepherd's field, from leading men to leading sheep. And he became a good shepherd. God has quite the sense of humor the way He works things out. It was as

Moses was watching his sheep, in other words, controlling his thoughts, did God illuminate him (burning bush) and the rest is history. So the point when God could use him was when he was being a good shepherd, (controlling his thoughts and emotions) watching his sheep. Until we become good shepherds ourselves, until we can obtain some reasonable control over our thoughts, our sheep, God can't use us to the fullest either, no matter where we are.

We all know the wonderfully noble parable of the lost sheep. The story where a shepherd would leave his whole flock to search for that one lost sheep to reunite him with the herd. This parable is multi-faceted, though written with a love theme behind it there was a much more practical reason why the shepherd would risk everything for sake of the one. When that little lamb or thought wanders off away from the protection of his shepherd, it is a sitting duck for all the predators that are out there and once that predator, be it a lion, tiger, or bear, gets a little taste of that lamb or thought it is sure to make him much bolder. That predator will not be satisfied to sit on the sidelines for long. It's had a taste and now your whole flock could be in danger. Usually when a lion or a bear comes around, a little shouting and rock throwing would suffice, but not once the predator has sampled the wares, you as a shepherd are going to have to deal with this issue in a much more face to face way, as David did in his younger days. This is all an analogy to what happens when as a Christian you let your mind stray into areas we are not supposed to. Once we have had a taste, watch out.

If you let that one bad thought, or sheep, out into the world (that sin will manifest itself) and the world becomes much bolder and more prevalent in your mind. Then you're in trouble! Be a good shepherd; don't let that baaaad little sheep or thought wander to far, for that is invitation for trouble that can all be avoided by taking the advice of the real Good Shepherd Jesus, and by taking into captivity all your thoughts, all of your emotions, all of your sheep. David was a good shepherd and God empowered him to do great things. Samuel 17:37 "David said moreover, the Lord that had delivered me out of the paw of the lion, and out of the paw of the bear, He will deliver me out of the hand of this Philistine (Goliath). Do we have any giant troubles in our lives, be the good shepherd and He will deliver you out of the hands of any giant problem you may encounter. David had gained some reasonable control, and David was used greatly by God.

David wrestled with the lion, fought with the bear that tried to attack his sheep. All that may have happened in the physical back in David's day but for us it means wrestling with our minds, and fighting off our bad thoughts. We're not going to fight with real animals anytime soon I hope. But just like a lion that can mortally wound you with one swipe, one erroneous thought can do the same. It only takes one stupid move on our part and we can ruin a marriage, a friendship, or even a business, one swipe. David by eventually learning how to be that good shepherd and gaining some control over his behavior was used greatly by God, though David like us was far from perfect. Contrary to what many people believe about sheep they are not a dumb animal. They could actually be trained to recognize their master's voice. In the winter shepherds would build pens in the mountains to coral all their sheep. Flocks would easily intermingle with other flocks, but when they heard their shepherd's voice they would recognize it and follow. Jesus said, "My sheep hear my voice "knowing people of that day would immediately understand what he was driving at. The big knock on sheep is that they are literally defenseless, they won't beat you to death with their shiny soft wool, or tear you apart with their flat grazing teeth so just like thoughts they need someone constantly watching over them. So we know that by slowly regaining control over thoughts, thoughts that would have previously gone unchecked, we are cleansing our minds and preparing ourselves for greater things. Being a good shepherd is putting ourselves in a position to be used by God. We need to recognize inharmonious thoughts such as anxiety, and fear, for just what they are, poisons and toxins to the body.

You wouldn't drink ammonia, or have a sulfuric acid sandwich but basically the same things happening with the same result. The only difference is one is much slower and subtle.

Okay, so how do we gain control over our thoughts both good and bad? How do we put into practice what we are talking about here? How do we become good shepherds of the mind? I hate to say it but this is one of the most clichéd answers of all time, still it is the only answer, Prayer. Pray about it, I've heard this so many times in my Christian walk. I almost shut-down when I hear it. But it's the truth. We hear it so often it is almost rendered useless. I'm not just talking about per functionary prayer, or casual prayer, as I call it I'm talking about a much deeper, intimate and therapeutic prayer. I'm talking about how Jesus prayed. Jesus made real contact, Jesus gave His undivided attention. Jesus would pray Himself directly into the presence of God. That's where the power is. He was always running off. Like Superman used telephone booths, Jesus would use the desert. He would use it to isolate Himself and get alone with God. He knew He had to get away from everything to be with the real most important thing (God). It is estimated that our minds process between 50 and 70,000 thoughts in a single day, a constant stream of electrical impulses telling our brains what to do, where to go, and what to say. It never stops. Even in our sleep this process continues on in our dreams. But we must make it stop. We need to stop the onslaught of thinking be it for even a little while. We must create for ourselves a gap then step into that gap, and there we'll find God. Slowing down the breathing, the heart rate, the blood pressure, will help us match frequencies with God. Be still and know, be still and hear, be still and receive.

Psalm 91:1 states "he that dwelleth in the Secret Place of the most high shall abide under the shadow of the Almighty". The secret place of the most high is your own consciousness, your own mind. Jesus said "When we were to pray we are to enter into the closet and shut the door" meaning to retire into thought within our own consciousness. Psalm 91 states that it is He that dwelleth in the Secret Place, not he that occasionally visits, runs in, and runs out, just to say hello. But it is he that dwelleth or spends time that shall abide under His shadow, or in other words receive His protection. True success in prayer depends on getting some degree of contact with God. You can't hurry it, can't put a time limit on it, you have to just let it happen. When Jesus said that we shall do greater things than even he did, in regards to miracles, healings, spiritual growth, it is in this gap we create, that those things shall happen. It is in this gap, where miracles exist, it is in this gap where we find God and where prayers are answered. Till we give God our undivided attention, till we shepherd our minds and lead our thoughts to Him, we miss the boat.

We are building a spiritual sanctuary or temple each time we visit Him on such a level. Stone by stone we must build a temple worthy of Him. Each time we dwelleth with Him in our consciousness we do that. We do this in silence. God said, "Be still and know that I am God". In the silence of your mind you must build a spiritual temple worthy of a king. Here's an interesting fact. King Solomon's temple possibly the most ornate and beautiful structures ever built that was dedicated solely to God as a place for Him to dwell with His people. This incredible wonder was built in silence. The same way your temple in your mind is built within the silence of prayer. 1 Kings 6:7 "and the house, when it was in building, was built of stone made ready before it was brought hither, so that there was neither hammer nor axe or any tool of iron heard in the house while it was in building. The palatal temple of Solomon was built in silence much like the temples in our mind.

Try this little visualization technique I use. Picture yourself standing in a beautiful field of gently swaying golden rods and spinning lilies of every color imaginable. The warm spring sun is caressing your face and a gentle breeze is massaging your back. You're in one of those special moments when time stands still and you allow yourself to appreciate the little things in life, a little bird sings his sweet song, only this time you listen, and almost know what its saying, you see a leaf being carried off by a bubbling brook and gaze at it till it floats from view wondering where it may end up. You look straight ahead and just off in the distance you see something you just can't believe, you squint and wipe your eyes but there it is directly ahead of you, unmistakable, you see Jesus. He is sitting on a rock surrounded by every animal you can imagine. There is a bluebird on His shoulder, a lamb sleeping in His lap and you remark to yourself how absolutely perfect and serene everything around Him is. You sense perfect harmony and long to partake in it. You only need to bridge that short distance between the two of you, your home, heaven itself awaits. But there is one problem one obstacle in your way between you and Jesus, between you and perfect harmony. There lies a road and on that road is a never ending procession of sheep. Yes sheep all sorts of sheep, big ones, little ones, black ones, white ones, every kind imaginable. They are herding by you at a breakneck speed. You try to cross but they beat you back, they are overwhelming and they don't stop. What is a person to do? Plain and simple, YOU MUST MAKE THEM STOP. You must step out on that road directly in front of that stream of sheep (thoughts) raise your hands up and say WHOA, enough is enough. Shut off that torrent of thinking be it only for a little while. Be that shepherd you were called to be and control that flock. Do not let it control you. Do not let anything keep you from your appointed time with Christ. Stop those sheep dead in their tracks, cross that road and sit down right by the side of the Savior Himself, and bath yourself in His glory. He will meet us there, we just need to create the space, the gap, walk in, shut the door, and sit down next to Him and give Him our all, not a piece or just a few minutes or what we can spare, but all our undivided attention. Listen, if you're in need of healing you have health issues be it mind or body, well God is health, He is not healthy, He is health itself vibrant and strong, why would you not want to sit with Him for a while? Draw from that perfect health He offers. Understand, to sit in the presence of God in prayer, you are being healed you are being affected in the most positive of ways. There is no better therapy on this planet.

Big decisions in your life need to be made, confused not sure which way to go, what to do, He is ultimate wisdom, He sees both beginning and end, why wouldn't you want to sit with Him for a while and ask His council and advice. He is there to place anything worthwhile into your life just for asking. Financial problems? Lonely? He is there in the gap. It is in the gap where miracles take place. Is there a temple in your mind for God? Have you built up a spiritual consciousness, worthy for Him to reside in? Will you give Him the time that is needed, will you meditate on Him and dwell with Him. The first step in developing this deeper connection with God is to truly dedicate the time that it takes, time that was never better spent. We must simply sit down, slow down our breathing, slow down our heart rate, lower our blood pressure and relax. We must "Be still and know He is God". Think of God review some of the things that you know to be true about Him. His perfect goodness, infinite intelligence, all presence and limitless power, unbounded love and so forth. Claim that God who is all those things is with you, and believe it. Say silently that you forgive everyone who may seem to need it without exception. Ask God to forgive you for all the mistakes you have made and say you accept His forgiveness, claim that God is now inspiring you, teaching you, healing you and leading you. Claim that He is giving you the greatest gift of all HIMSELF because having Him you will have everything else worthwhile. Giving thanks in advance for the peace of mind, the harmony and spiritual growth that is yours. When you finally leave that rendezvous with God that gap, you'll be different, you'll be better. You'll be healed.

I'm So Confused?

Have you ever had your head spinning over all the different factions and directions that today's so called organized religions can take you. We have starring in alphabetical order, the Assemblies of God, the Amish, the Atheist, the Seven day Adventist. We have the Baptists, the Anna Baptist, the Fundamentalist Baptists, Catholics, Santa Marian Catholics, Byzantine Catholics, and Roman Catholics. We have the Christian Scientist, the Church of Christ, the Congregationalist, the United Congregationalist, the Episcopal, the Federated church, the United Federated, the non-Denominational. You have Lutherans, Orthodox Christians, Pentecostals, Presbyterians, Quakers, United Methodists, Unitarians, and Unitarian Universalists. These are the ones with a Christian slant to them. Let us not forget the rest of the World. We also have Judaism, Zionism, Islamists, and Kabbalist. Throw in Buddhism, Confucianism, Hinduism and top it off with the humanistic views and Satanic Worship. Wow. The really sad part is that all these different factors have warring parties within themselves jockeying for position with a myriad of dissenting opinions and fractured leadership. They all seem to possess that fundamental exclusivity clause that states that their way is the only way and everyone else is wrong. They would rather dig their heels in and fight with everyone else rather than find common ground and work together. What the exclusionists in religion do not see, is that he shuts the door to heaven on himself in striving to shut others out. More deaths, more wars, more pain and anguish have been caused by religious extremists than any other cause including the inexhaustible thirst for gold and property. In today's day and age terrorism has reached and stained our very shores and our national security will never be the same. What is one to do? What is one to think? I myself personally have never been of the type to just except outright what I've been taught. I question everything, not with a disproving attitude or negativity, but with an open mind and a tremendous thirst for truth. I know intuitively that there is no box that can contain the Creator of the Universe, no Baptist box, no Catholic box, no Buddhist box. God is infinite. God is too big to be defined, too big to be exclusively owned by any one organization, or any one cultures view. I am a respecter of all religions, for who am I to be judge and jury to things outside my own sphere of life and knowledge. I can't speak Chinese, so who am I to speak for the Chinese. Being of a Western culture would seem to limit me to a certain line of thinking and living, unless one takes a step outside that limited scope and begins to study the world at large. We need a world view of life, not a segregated one. I have spent a better part of my life studying and looking at all the different major religions this world has to offer. I have studied Buddhism and found God there; I have studied Islam, and the Koran, and found God there also. I've read Emerson and Tinsdale, Socrates, and Polonius and low and behold God was there also.

I've searched the whole world and all of time for God and His truth and found it in varying degrees everywhere. All that searching and questioning, literally decades of it, has led me full circle right back to where I originally started, right back to my own personal roots in Christianity and Jesus Christ. God is Omni present and everywhere, He is in China, in Taiwan, in Brazil, in America, and in your hometown, as well as in your own heart. Trying to claim God as all your own or that He speaks the truth only thru your religious preference is ludicrous and simply ego centered thinking. I also know that trying to tell someone that if they are not ready to hear it is ludicrous also but here goes, God belongs to everyone and everyone belongs to God. God has placed His spirit liberally in everyone, but it is up to each of us individually to fully recognize this fact, to awaken and to cultivate that spiritual power within. God does not love the Anglo Saxon Christian, more than the Eastern Asian Buddhist. God simply loves, and just as any parent would want to see his children grow in light, and love, wherever they may have been planted. Pure love as possessed by God has no restrictions, no boundaries, and no territories. God's love is a force a power open to all of humanity. In saying that and in studying the different expressions of God found all over the world, I would have to admit that some of Gods revelations or teachings are far more evolved and refined than others. God reaches people at their own level of understanding hence forth we have varying degrees of illumination. The teachings of Jesus Christ rest on a higher plane. Jesus's teachings elevate and illuminate to a whole new level. I do not come to this conclusion because I was taught it. This statement is not a product of my heritage or upbringing it is a culmination of much questioning, earnest seeking and Godly guidance. Jesus Christ son of God, son of man, truly deserves title as the Savior of the World. No matter how you may wish to define Him, God, Prophet or fanatic, Jesus Christ is unquestionably the most influential and important figure to ever grace the stage of mankind. The life and death of Jesus Christ and all the revelations attributed to Him have influenced the course of human history more so than any other that has ever lived. No one, not Caesar, not Churchill, not our own founding fathers can even hold a candle to Him or His impact. Jesus has been the guide post, the light, the path for all of Western civilization and Europe for two thousand years. Shaping us politically, socially, culturally. His message, His teachings, His views have circled the globe, altering the destiny of the entire world. No one outranks Him in world prominence and influence, no one is even close. Why do I say Jesus's teachings are so revolutionary, so evolved, and so much higher? Why would I put them on a higher plane than other great spiritual teachers of our time. It's easy once you've studied them, for Jesus's teachings advanced the cause, the evolution, the advancement of mankind by tenfold. We have had two thousand years to absorb and implement the import received from Jesus Christ. I cannot even imagine what the world would be like today without His intercession on behalf of mankind. We as a people, as a race, have come a long way but hence still have a long way to go. Our maturity level spiritually is probably around the pre-toddler stage. Jesus being our model our prototype shows us what we are to become, shows us our inevitable potential as human and spiritual beings. I praise Him every day for His example, for the benchmark He has set. Jesus's oneness with God, the power He received thru deep meditation prayer, opened Him up to truth no man at that time possessed. He taught practical methods for the development of one's soul. There are no rituals or theology in His teaching, these were added later by well intentioned, but misguided religious leaders of the day. He taught principles only not rules or regulations. He seemed doggedly anti-ecclesiastical, and was constantly at war with the religious leaders of the day. What really concerned Jesus was the character of one's soul, not their religious affiliation or position in life. He taught the art of prayer, and the fact that prayer really does change things. To Him prayer is not whimsical, it's not fairy tale like, and it simply works when approached correctly. It is in of itself a force, and a power given unto mankind, yet mankind still to this day on the whole knows it not. Today I want to look at two aspects of His teachings which convince me beyond a shadow of a doubt that "He and the Father were one", that Jesus is the key that unlocks our inner temple, and spills forth the fact that you're true self is a child of God. You are but a spark off the torch of the Creator. Jesus's light was so bright he changed the world. He pioneered a whole new approach to God that was both intensely personal and relevant at the same time. Jesus taught well outside of His cultural influence, and His revelations were just that revelations. Even two thousand years later he is still way ahead of His time.

Jesus My Super Hero

Today in our culture we have many, many, super heroes. We have Batman, Superman, Iron Man, Wonder Woman, the Fantastic Four and many more celluloid fictional characters that our youth, awe and marvel at. They are always at work saving the world from its arch nemesis and a full array of evil doers. They never seem to sleep and are always wary, watching the backs of us ordinary citizens. What would we do without them?

Theodore White a political writer earlier this century wrote "To go against the dominant thinking of your friends, of your time, of most of the people you see every day is perhaps the most difficult act of heroism you can have". I would have to agree.

Jesus did just that. Jesus taught both outside of His cultural influence and way beyond His time period. His teachings were not the rehashing of previous ideas, He did not build upon the foundation of others, for his teachings were totally unique and original. They were cutting edge for his day and remain so even in our day.

Jesus refused to conform to the world at large no Jesus would make the world conform to Him. Jesus was all about evolution, not biological for that will take care of itself but spiritual. The spiritual evolution of the soul was His game, and He will eventually and undoubtedly win. For nonconformity the world whips you with its displeasure. The world did not stop at whipping Jesus for His radical thinking it would all culminate in death for Him, for His ideas rattled the very institutions of His day. Jesus simply made it personal. And in an act of self-preservation by the religious of the day, nails were struck in both hands and feet. To be great is to be misunderstood for greatness always appeals to the future.

The greatest problem today with our fractured Christianity and diversity of opinion is that the leaders, the priests, or the pastor has pledged himself to look at but one side, the permitted side, not as a child of God but as a church official. Emerson describing such men said "He is like a retained attorney and I already know ahead of time that nothing new or spontaneous can come from him". He is paid to spout the company line. When his institution has peaked he has peaked and progress goes no further.

Jesus Christ by stepping outside of the confines of religious authority renovated all of life for all of man, for all of time. He single handedly catapulted man into a whole new realm of existence. The only influence seen or felt in His teaching is that of God Himself and that is where His genius lies. His truths are recognized intuitively by our spirits and we are gladly led by them. His teaching when allowed resonate with our hearts confirm our weak hands from shaking and our knees from knocking.

Make no mistake about it, we are all products of our cultural heritage and we are all products of the time period in history that we live. It is not always easy to divorce ourselves from the influences good or bad that these traits hold for us. Our food, our families, our thinking, has been shaped and molded by the outside in, by habitat, and family and love of country, all the while slowly tightening the noose of objective and impartial thinking. Only a world view of things can open one's eyes. Only a world view of things can make us see all the tremendous blessings all around us. Only a world view allows us to appreciate all that we have while at the same time acquiring a compassion for those not in the same position as we are.

You have no idea how much your family, your town, your religious affiliation; your education has solidified and molded you both good and bad. If you are not careful you can drown yourself in all these persuasions and never know the real you. We must poke our head up above these waters of limitation and breathe the air of freedom as Jesus did; the air of freedom is the very breathe of God.

Listen with intent to God first, your mother and father second. God first and the politician second, God first and your secular teachers second. We cannot justify ourselves in the eyes of others for then we become just a "cog in the machine" and the man himself is lost. Our justification is found in Him.

This is what places Jesus discourses on a higher level and newer spiritual plane. Jesus taught both outside of His culture and well beyond His time period. Culturally in Jesus day women were second class citizen's, possessions of their husbands left at home to do household work and menial chores. They were looked upon as subservient sexual subjects, slaves of both their time and culture. Jesus would have none of that.

Jesus taught that all men and all women are equal in the sight of God. We as a nation have just gotten around to recognizing woman's rights as being equal and on par with men. It is just within the last half century that we see women with the right to vote, with the right to enter the workplace on level footing with the male. Women are just now starting to stretch the muscle of inalienable rights.

Intrinsic rights denied them for centuries are just availing themselves years after Christ death and resurrection. The seed that helped facilitate all this advancement was planted by Jesus many harvests ago. Jesus being above His culture and outside His time period, just naturally treated women as equals. It was unheralded and distasteful to the orthodox religious of the day. In the face of all opposition Jesus treated all women that He came in contact with, respect, love, and reverence.

This was unheard of in first century Palestine but this was the genius of Jesus. The first person the newly resurrected Jesus spoke to and revealed Himself to was a woman, Mary Magdalene. The first command given out by the Savior Jesus was to her also whom He commissioned to go and tell the brethren what she saw.

This speaks volumes by itself. Jesus's only influence was direct from God Himself no cultural edicts could sway Him for He was a direct revelation from God. Paul writer of two thirds of the New Testament, possessor of the Christ consciousness, a giant in the eyes of religion, he himself couldn't escape all his cultural influences.

Paul continually felt the need to keep women in their place. There is a subtle underlying angst when it comes to women in his writings that hard to ignore. I do not say this to lay Paul low, but to underscore the pure divinity in Jesus's way. Jesus soared above His culture for His culture was of God and not of this earthly plane.

Jesus's teachings were way ahead of His time period, in His day you were either a farmer, shepherd, craftsman or soldier. Males ruled because they were bigger and stronger. Fighting in that day was a very personal thing, you looked your victims in the eyes as you thrust your sword or knife in his heart, you needed a bow and arrow to shoot someone from a distance, for guns were not invented yet. Death was very up close and personal.

Violence and brute strength ruled the day. Gladiators, cheered on by the crowds, would cut their enemies to pieces to the delight of the spectators. The arena was their entertainment. Spilled blood was a gift, a treat given to the masses to quench their ferocious appetites and appease their brutal natures. These same Gladiators were treated as gods much like our spoiled super star athletes of the day. This was the norm. This was the way of the times. So when Jesus stood up and preached against the sickness of violence that gripped the people He was not tickling their ears or telling them what they wanted to hear. He was standing directly in a fierce wind of opposition a true social tempest.

People of that time loved the games, loved the blood much like people of today love their football, love their hockey, and love their boxing. Jesus standing before a throng of people only to say if someone strikes you turn the other cheek, or if someone steals your shirt offer them your coat, was absolutely unheard of. This line of thinking was suicidal to them. They could not sense the subtle power behind it. It was submissive and defeatist, for they did not yet grasp the all-encompassing power of love. Love in those days was not looked upon as a force, force was looked upon as a force.

Totally foreign and totally new and totally of God it would seem He was preaching weakness but in reality He was teaching the ultimate strength. Jesus was working the mind of the people, the very psyche of the human race. He was trying to bring about a change in their consciousness, in their thinking for without that change of consciousness nothing of any permanence would occur. This seed He planted would grow very slowly at first, taking centuries to do its work but it has grown.

Moses gave us the commandment, "thou shall not kill". To an early primitive barbaric race this was better than nothing. If this edict kept two people or a group of people from killing themselves over something trivial all the well and good. It was a start a new beginning. Moses was more concerned at this time with the people's actions rather than their motives. When raising young children you try to give them simple commands nothing to confusing and once they get a handle on the simpler things we move on to the more complicated.

At the perfect time in history Jesus came to address the mind, to raise it to a new level of consciousness. It wasn't enough not to just refrain yourself from killing Jesus said you can't even hate your neighbor. To hate your neighbor and not kill him wasn't good enough. Jesus wanted to take humanity to the next level. He wants us now to look inward, to look at our motives and reasoning. Jesus says to even harbor thoughts of hate is detrimental to both you and your neighbor.

Eye for an eye and a tooth for a tooth just would not cut it anymore, it was time to evolve. Jesus was ushering in a new era, vigilante justice, getting even, revenge all those are primitive instincts and ways of aggression. To return evil for evil, hate with hatred is the start of a vicious never ending cycle that mankind to this day has yet to escape. Jesus goes right into the mind, the psyche and says "resist not evil" do not antagonize a situation for in doing so you only give it power. For curses you are to return blessings and hatred you are to reward with love. Do not wrestle with emotions such as hatred and revenge for "Revenge is mine saith the Lord". Let God balance the situation, for when you withdraw any negative energy you may have initially wanted to give it, the situation will fade into nothingness.

Right reaction is the supreme secret of life. Jesus knew that with any kind of difficulty it is the reaction that you give it mentally, the attitude that you adopt toward it that determines its effect on you. It is the application of Love, "the ultimate force" against which no evil can stand. Jesus was placing mankind on the high road, the spiritual path once trodden, there is no going back.

Conclusion

This outer world that we live in is far from being the prison of circumstances that it is commonly thought to be. Phrases such as "that's my lot" or "those are just the cards I'm dealt" melt away in insignificance when we realize the truth. Truth being that your whole outer world of experience, your life has no character of its own whatsoever good or bad. The only character it has is what you give it. It is essentially a blank canvas molding itself to your own thoughts. It is not foisted upon you. It is you who create it.

Throughout your life all the thoughts that occupy your mind are molding your destiny be it good or bad and that the whole of your life experiences is but the outer manifestation of your inner thoughts. You are in control for it is you and only you that pick the thoughts that you entertain. Your quality of life is in your hands. Your life is truly your responsibility.

The good news is if you have made it a mess up to this point you can change it. Your life is of your ordering, we reap what we have sown. Many of us do this totally unconsciously. We have free will but our free will lies in the choices of our thinking. Listen if you really do wish to change your life to become a different person altogether in the sight of God and man then take Jesus's teaching to heart (mind). Once the true meaning of Jesus's instructions are grasped, and implanted in one's life, it is only a matter of time before you will receive practical, life changing direction.

If you really do want Health, Peace of mind and spiritual development then Jesus is the way. The task is not an easy one but it can be done. Each one of us must do our own work, no one but you can save you, and with the power of Practical Christianity, and Jesus Christ Himself you can to be victorious. Make your life what you want it, dictate to it, and don't let it dictate you. That is your dominion that you have been promised, take advantage of it for the time is at hand. This is the God given power of your mind, use it wisely. As we learn step two of this symbiotic dance (mind) of human existence, let's use it in conjunction with step one the body and know with confidence and assuredness that we are two thirds of the way there of firing on all cylinders. Remember as a man thinketh so he is.

"Call No Man Common Or Unclean"

Instead of using God's word, His teachings, to broaden our mind, to open you up to all kinds of new possibilities in life many have used it to do quite the opposite. We have used it to narrow ourselves, to hem ourselves in to a certain line of thinking. To exclude anyone who wasn't raised as we were, who weren't taught the same things as I.

If we allow this tunnel vision into our spiritual lives it will breed a certain type of elitism, a chosen race mentality that has stricken this planet into a partial paralysis. We as a people, we learn very slowly, but we do learn.

We call ourselves Christians, we use and invoke Jesus's name, but until we have honestly looked inside ourselves, revised everything within then sadly we are not. We have inherited all sorts of prejudices from our families, from our nations, from our schools and worst of all from our churches. Revision is Growth though we know it not. In Acts 10:1-55 we find the apostle Peter being taught by God Himself to revise some of His long held beliefs.

Peter though serving with Jesus for over three years, converting himself over to this new religion Christianity, and called upon to spread this new message of change around the globe was still very much an orthodox Jew. Jews considered themselves the chosen race but we know now there is no such thing. We are all just pieces of one big puzzle. It takes all of us to make it whole.

No race is any better or favored more than another. God created us all equal. Moses and the Jews were chosen to carry forth His word because on the whole, in the early days of the Bible, they had stayed away from idolatry, kept the sanctity of their women, and maintained a certain purity and cleanliness of their homes, better than any of the other nations of their day. They also had Moses. Moses was unique not because he was a Jew, all the individual races have their geniuses, their prodigies, their prophets, but because he answered the call in his life, that made him unique, because most of us plain and simply don't. We hear the bell but fail to rise.

The Israelites had chosen God so God chose them. They were fickle and frustrating but God stuck with them. The only chosen races are people anywhere in the world that earnestly seek Him and do His will. If you whole heartedly seek His face, honestly strive to do His will, you are of the chosen race. It can be dangerous when a nation erroneously copies this elitist attitude of superiority.

The Germans in the 40's felt the white Asian race was superior and we all know what atrocities happened next. The French under Napoleon made the same mistake and many people believe by joining a certain church, or associating with a certain group will mean their salvation but of course it doesn't. Here in Acts Peter is about to learn as we all should that we should not call any man common or unclean, we shouldn't hide behind nationalistic pride to scourge another nation, or another person, and that what God has cleansed "call not thou common".

There was a certain man in Caesarea called Cornelius a centurion of the band called the Italian band. A devout man and one that feared (revered) God with all his heart. He gave much alms to the people and prayed to God always. For this God honored him. He was visited by an angel of God and commanded to send men to Joppa a seaside village and to call upon one man Simon Peter. Cornelius being curious and obedient sent three men on their way to locate this Simon Peter.

Peter in the meantime went up to the rooftop of the house he was staying at to pray, about the sixth hour he became very hungry but before eating fell into a trance. Acts 11: He saw the heavens open up and a certain vessel descending unto him, as it had been a great sheet knit at the four corners and let down to earth. Acts 12: Wherein were all manner of four footed beasts of the earth and creeping things, and fowls of the air. And there came a voice unto him "Rise Peter kill and eat".

Here's where the lesson starts. Peter had much to learn or should I say unlearn. God is telling him to eat the foods that he had been taught were unclean. God was repealing what was one of the strictest of the Mosaic Laws, the laws about diet. These laws, these rituals had out grown themselves they were intended for a particular body of people the Jews, in a specific time span early AD, in a particular desert climate. They were doubtlessly necessary at that time but had out grown their relevance and usefulness. Peter's vision told him that there was nothing sacred about diet, to eat whatever seemed appropriate and available. God spoke to Peter and said "what God hath cleansed, don't you call common"!!!! This was reiterated 3 times to Peter.

In one stroke all the artificial laws of the Pentateuch were wiped out. Jesus put it simply and clearly, it is not what goes into the mouth that defiles a person, (it is not what you eat that matters), it is what cometh out of the mouth, your thoughts and words that matter.

Peter's life was being (revised, updated) for him, an apostle of the Lord should not harbor prejudices, and this lesson was about to get much deeper and personal for him. This lesson is not just for him, it is for all of us. We all must from time to time reassess our thoughts and grow. If we have not had any great revelations in our lives lately we are not growing. If some new thought or inspiration hasn't blown you away lately, you're not looking very hard.

You cannot reach a point of satisfaction, when it comes to your spiritual progress there is always something to learn or relearn for that matter. There can be no stagnation. Peter was about to learn one of the most powerful lessons in his life. Peter was willing to listen he was up to the challenge. Are you?

Now while Peter doubted in himself exactly what this vision he had seen should mean behold the men which were sent by Cornelius stood before the gate of the house inquiring about Peter. Peter still contemplating on the vision heard from God again saying "behold three men seek thee, arise and go with them, for I have sent them".

The men explained themselves as being sent by Cornelius and the next day the group headed back to Caesarea. As Peter approached Cornelius met him, fell down at his feet and worshiped him, but Peter took him up saying, "Stand up for I myself also am only a man".

They entered the house and found many different kinds of people had gathered together. Here now is where lesson number two begins for Peter, and all of us. Peter still under the influence of being an orthodox Jew, looking at things through this narrow prism of prejudice said to them "You know how that it is an unlawful thing for a man that is a Jew to keep company or to enter the home of one of another nation".

Can you say prejudice, can you say discrimination can you see the direction that God is leading Peter in. Peter being told earlier by God that he was not to look down upon or snub his nose at anything that God has cleansed in regards to the old views of diet was now teaching him the same lesson, except now this lesson is directed toward our relationships with people.

He is being told to mix with other people he is being told to throw away his old attitudes of superiority and elitism to put away his national pride and stop being judgmental and to open the door of his heart to anyone regardless of color, race or ethnicity. The Jewish people were caught up in a false sense of national pride. It had always been "them against the world" and they held great value to their Hebrew roots.

They considered themselves the very physical descendants of Abraham. They were the chosen people. So imagine how

Peter felt when God was telling him that it all meant nothing and that the truth is that if anyone of any color, of any race, of any creed seeks to put God first in their lives, such as Cornelius, then they are of the chosen race, they are a child of God and should be treated as such. Respected, revered and welcomed as a brother.

God chooses those who choose Him. God helps those who help themselves. All this rains down on Peter like a ton of bricks, his enlightenment comes and he speaks the words that should pierce the heart of anyone that hears them, "God has shown me that I should not call any man common or unclean". Peter revised all his thinking that day, put away all his prejudices and proceeded to do what God had commanded him to do all along. God wanted Peter to bring his words to life, to make an example of himself and that is just what Peter did.

Feed my sheep, spread the word, and love one another as yourself. Cooperate, learn from one another, see the good in one another fit all the pieces of the puzzle together, but most of all "Love the Lord thy God with all thy heart and love ALL your neighbors as yourself". Cornelius so excited that he has an 'apostle of the Lord' at his doorstep said to the waiting group, "We are all here present before God to hear all things that are commanded thee of God". Peter never had such an eager and open minded audience for it was not a room of racially mixed people, it was a room of thirsty souls longing for the Word.

Then Peter opened his mouth and said these famous words, "Of a truth I perceive that God is no respecter of persons". God doesn't look at your color, God doesn't look at your religion God doesn't look at your position in life God looks only at your heart. Peter ends this personal transformation this revision in his life, with these words direct from God. "But in every nation" (do you hear that, every nation) he that feareth God and worketh righteousness is accepted with Him. If God accepts a man any man under these terms then how dare you call any man common or unclean. No race of people dominates another, we have individuals within each race that excel and dominate in certain areas but God is all about balance and polarity. He forces us to need one another or as a people we will never be complete.

We must learn and feed off each other, we must use all the pieces of the puzzle to get a glimpse of the whole picture. For anyone seeking God with all his heart, no matter where he is from, or where he is at is a child of God and of the chosen race.

One of the greatest teachings the world has ever received comes from Jesus's discourses in The Sermon on the Mount. Jesus's teachings were so revolutionary, so ground breaking, so provoking He felt the need before He even began to preface it with a cautionary trailer like we see sometimes at the movies or at carnival rides. This experience may be too intense for younger viewers, or you must be at least this age and this height to ride this ride.

Jesus wasn't changing anything in scripture but He was going to take us deeper than we've ever been and in doing so felt the need to say to those who would accuse Him of superseding the Mosaic Law, Matt 5:17-18 "Do not think that I have come to abolish the law or the Prophets, I have not come to abolish them but to fulfill them. (to deepen your thinking of them).

I tell you the truth until heaven and earth disappear, not the smallest letter, not the last stroke of a pen, (not a jot or a tittle if you prefer the King James Version) will by any means disappear from the Law until everything is accomplished. Jesus wasn't changing the laws of Moses, (our laws) He was deepening the width, the breadth, and the height of those commandments. He was internalizing them for us pointing out that the motives behind the actions were as important as the actions themselves.

Verse 20, For I tell you unless your righteousness (right thinking) surpasses that of the Pharisees and the teachers of the law you will certainly not enter into the kingdom of heaven.

Matt 5:21, You have heard that it was said to the people long ago (Moses) Do not murder, and anyone who murders will be subject to the judgment. Jesus revises this a little when He says, "but I tell you anyone who is even angry with his brother will be subject to the judgment". Jesus says it is not enough just to restrain yourself from killing someone you must restrain your mind from the anger which leads to the wanting to kill in the first place. He doesn't alter the law, Jesus deepens it and brings it inside.

Matt 27: You have heard it said of old (Moses) Do not commit adultery, but I tell you, "that anyone who has even looked upon a women lustfully has already committed adultery with her in his heart (mind). Jesus widened it and connects it to thought. Jesus was attacking the thinking behind it not just the act itself. Jesus knows the thought is the very root of the action.

Matt 38, You have heard it said of old (Moses) "Eye for an eye and a tooth for a tooth", but Jesus updated this with but I tell you, "Do not even resist an evil person". Turn the other cheek. Jesus of course knowing violence just breeds more violence no matter how justified we may feel follows that up with Matt 43 "Ye have heard said of old time, Thou shall love thy neighbor and hate thine enemy, But I say unto you, Love your enemies, bless them that curse you, do good to those that hate you and pray for them that despisefully use you and persecute you.

Why, "that ye may be the children of your Father which is in heaven". To be a child of God is to look at and reverse all those things in your life that don't line up with the Word. Your Father which is in heaven loves His enemies and does not call any man unclean or common. But in every nation he that feareth God and worketh righteousness is accepted by Him.

Look inside your heart, your mind, see if we may be holding on to some old ways of thinking, some handed down prejudices or unwanted anger toward anyone or anything. For you may have heard of old, but Jesus says, Revise and call no man common.

Soul

Let Us Make Man In Our Image

God opened His heart, His soul and His mind to mankind when He said the words in Genesis 1:26 "Let us make man in our image, in our likeness". God flung open His arms and embraced humanity. He welcomed us into His fold making these beyond a doubt the greatest words ever uttered, for with these words a link was forged, a bond was set and a personal relationship with deity itself became possible. Without these words we would be mere shadows of ourselves. We would be obscured in diversity in the great pageantry of this planet.

With these words, "Let us make man in our image", we were given the ability to deeply reason, to grasp abstract concepts and to hone them into tools. To learn and expand upon all that this planet has to offer and then go beyond into the celestial, the heavens themselves, That is what man, (somewhat unconsciously) has been trying to do all these past centuries. With these words we entered into an eternal relationship with the Creator and all of His creation. A deep mystical bond and an ever deepening relationship that time holds no chains too. He elevated mankind above the rest of His incredible creation and put us on a spiritual pedestal, high above all else. He partnered with man and we should always be eternally grateful. That is why we were chosen. God is ultimate intelligence and these words, "Let us make man in our image" blessed us with a shadow of that intelligence, a shadow of His infinite perfection and total completeness. Our job is to bring that shadow to light by reflecting His image. We reflect His image when we use our intelligence to advance God's qualities and desires.

On this earth mankind is in a class by itself, not on his own merit, or by his own doings, but by God's inclusion in His family. We win by default. God chose humanity to place His divine spark, God chose humanity to individualize Himself in each of us, to separate us from the strictly natural side of life, and place us into the eternal, the spiritual and the everlasting side.

To make man in our image was to place or to infuse within us a seed, a very real piece of God Himself. This seed and I pray it reaches fertile ground is your soul. It is your greatest possession. It is useless to try to quantify the soul in terms we may understand, language has no chance, but some say it is a type of pure energy, an etheric saturation, a field of energy encompassing the entire physical body.

Regardless of how you may try to describe it, it remains out of reach in human tongue, for who could describe something that allows you to commune with the Divine and speak the language of God. Your soul allows you access into the world of spirit, the world of God and all its inherent powers. It is not contingent on joining a certain church or the reciting of a certain creed. There are no strings attached. It is truly freely given. It lifts you out of the constraints of this earthly existence and places you on the path of unlimited potential. Potential revealed to us most clearly in the personage of Jesus Christ. Potential beyond what any of us can imagine or dream of, real potential and true power, a vivid realization of my immortal being and my unique parentage.

We must understand and realize that God is not in some far off place, "He is not up in the sky sitting on a throne in heaven arbitrarily watching mankind unfold". He is a personal inward and intimate presence closer to us than hands and feet. Make no mistake about it God is a hands on kind of guy, He will tinker, He will adjust, only of course if we allow Him.

God sealed Himself within with this seed we call our soul. Nothing can separate us from His love. We can choose to ignore, we can look the other way, but His Divine presence is always there, tugging, urging, silently leading. Communion with the spirit is one of the greatest privileges in life, and prayer is everything. God is my most trusted companion. His Spirit is my Spirit. Jesus stated, "I and my Father are one". With this understanding Jesus places us on our own path of oneness, our own attuning to God. Jesus's oneness with God, His wisdom, His strength, was fueled through prayer. Prayer is the very cornerstone of spiritual life, so utterly fundamental yet so totally undiscovered by the world at large. It is a practice, a talent, a discipline, once implemented will change every aspect of your life automatically. Once you have attained true personal contact through prayer there is no going back there could be no greater wholeness or a more complete oneness.

If I allow it to it will direct my thoughts to all positive possibilities in life, it will steer my actions into meaningful channels of self-expression it will unite me with an all sustaining love. Godly affection and deep lasting relationships will mark my life. It will make my path perfect and straight, and always clearly before me, my sorrow is turned to gladness, my shame replaced with exhortation and my tears shall evaporate with the light of His glorious Spirit.

We have holidays to commemorate veterans, we have holidays to mark the beginning and ending of summer, we have ethnic holidays and religious holidays. We have national holidays to celebrate everything from Thanksgiving to our nation's independence. All well and good, but I believe that we should have a worldwide holiday, a celebration of celebrations honoring the Day the Lord, God looked down upon the earth, cast His gaze toward it lovingly and said, "it was good, it was very good", and then looked down upon man and said,

(Gen.1:26) "Let us make man in our image, in our likeness, and let them rule over all the earth".

Do we as a people, Do we as a race, really even began to fathom the implications of that statement. Can we grasp the scope of such a sweeping revelation as this? I'm sorry to say this but, the greater majority of this human race does not, for if we did, the first thing we would do every morning would be to fall on our faces and thank the Lord for adopting us into His own.

We are a royal priesthood, sons and daughters of the Most High, positioned to grow and evolve in His image and likeness. He chose us to be the caretakers of this incredible creation of His. He tells us to be fruitful and multiply, fill the earth and subdue it.

He chose us to delegate some of His supreme authority in the developing of this planet called earth. He chose which means He had a choice, and we should be eternally grateful that the choice was man. As humans we must be aware that we share this world with all the miraculous creations we find listed in the first six days of creation.

We share the earth with the beautiful blue sky. Who could argue at the breathtaking artistry of God with each and every sunset, the color and hues are beyond stunning, stirring within us new hope for each new day. Each night is an ending and each morning a new beginning. That beautiful blue sky is really a paper thin atmospheric sliver that gives you the very air you need to breathe, protection from our fiery friend the sun, and even waters on cue the entire planet for us can't ask for more than that. Let's ask ourselves a question, how well are we doing as a race, fulfilling our responsibility as caretakers in that department. If trends aren't reversed, that delicate little balancing act going on right above your head may be damaged beyond repair. It's a sick shame what we have done to our atmosphere and what we continue to do, all in the name of profit. These are problems left unchecked simply no amount of money or profit can rectify.

We share this planet with the seas, and all the living creatures within. This book is being written during the Deep Water Horizon oil leak into the gulf, hundreds of millions of gallons of pure crude oil have leaked into our oceans killing tens of thousands of marine animals and decimating the aquatic life. Elsewhere ocean temperatures slowly rise and one of the most important ocean wonders (coral) are slowly dying off. The negative chain reactions are untold and hopefully they are reversible We will never know the complete negative impact so I'd say we definitely failed and continue to fail in that department also.

We share this planet with other entities and maybe we haven't been the best caretakers yet but we still have time. God chose us. He saw in us something that maybe we don't see in ourselves, but He did see something and God doesn't make mistakes.

How did God separate us from the pack? How did He make us in His image? He placed within us a soul and in doing so made us miraculous. We all are aware of the physical side of life, the senses, the feelings, human need but the soul allows us participation in the spiritual side of life, one we never could or would have known about outside of our soul.

The soul gives man creativity and vision, for without it there would be no advancement. Our mere human minds are so limited outside the scope of the soul. The soul breeds our inspiration, our curiosity. God is ultimate intelligence and we can tap this unlimited reservoir of wisdom and knowledge not because of our minds but undoubtedly due to our souls, our cosmic connection.

Our souls make us in His image and His image is limitless intelligence and endless inspiration. Without our souls we would have no original creativity, we would have no great works of art, or great works of engineering. No Michelangelo's, or Raphael's, no Einstein's or Plato's. All of man's greatest works and discoveries pour thru his soul. Masterpieces are made by the Master. It's the dashes of Divinity we see in all the great works of art, which makes them resonate so strongly within.

The timeless treasures are works of Gods hand and His beauty shines thru them all. From the spark of a fire to the ring of a cell phone, it's all of God and His genius. Thomas Edison did not create electricity it has always been all around us for all of time. The Romans could have had light bulbs, instead of lanterns. God allowed Edison's mind to formulate, to tinker and to discover Gods incredible bounty, His power, but without His soul Edison himself wouldn't have even looked. He would have remained in the dark.

All of man's great accomplishments in all areas of life from society to science, are gifts of God unveiled to us sometimes through our minds but definitively because of our souls.

Psalm 8: David writes "when I consider your heavens the works of your fingers, the moon and the stars, which you have set in place, what is man that you are so mindful of Him"? What is man, man is a miraculous creation specifically tailored to live on this planet, as caretakers, as partners, as sons and daughters, all validated by our souls. What is man? We are His image, His embodiment, His representatives down here and that is reason to celebrate. Reason surely for a holiday.

Ultimately there is no limitation we can't beat. No limitations on our future. What is man that you are so mindful of Him? Ralph Waldo Emerson breaths beauty with the words of his soul when he says in his essay the Over Soul, "what we commonly call man, the eating, the drinking, the planting and the counting man does not as we know him represent himself; but misrepresents himself.

Him we do not respect, but the soul whose organ he is, would he let it appear through his action, would make our knees bend. When it breathes through His intellect, it is genius, when it breathes through His will, it is virtue, when if flows through His affection, it is love. All reform aims, is someone particular to let the great soul have its way through us, in other words to engage us to obey".

Of this pure nature every man is at some time sensible. Language cannot paint it with its color; it is too subtle. It is indefinable, immeasureable but we know that it pervades and contains us!

I would employ that everybody read that essay called the Over Soul, for in all of literature this is the closest I feel that the soul has been captured in words and description. When you have finished it you can't help but be left in a tremendous sense of awe; of the wisdom, virtue, power and beauty of this organ we call the soul.

The soul is the perceiver and revealer of truth and because of it we are wiser than we know. Let the cynic and the scoffer say what they will, when your spirit hears the truth it responds to it. Truth resounds within you, you may read an entire book or sit through a long fiery sermon and yet only a few precious points remain lodged in your mind, like a faint and wispy echo ringing off in the clouded distance stirring you, evoking you, calling your name.

Emanuel Swedenberg put it so aptly in his statement "It is no proof of a man's understanding to be able to affirm whatever he please, but to be able to discern that what is true is true and that what is false is false, this is the mark and character of intelligence".

The soul is the revealer of truth, it speaks in revelations. It encompasses the highest forms of communication, so subtle, so meek. The lies the misconceptions of this life the soul acts as a surgeon skillfully removing what does not belong, rebuilding what is in disrepair, ultimately healing the entirety. We shall make them in our image.

God standing before the looking glass and sees back only Love, Truth, Perfection, let these attributes invade you, let them be your tongue and mode of communication for they are the higher elements of life, very fleeting if you are not diligently seeking.

They are not monopolized by the educated or the learned or religious, but given freely to all, to the rich man, and the poor from the high to the low. To you and to me in whatever portion we seek. We are all discerning spirits.

(In many aspects our souls mirror our minds). Our minds are our rudders directing our paths here on earth. Our souls are our rudders directing our paths through eternity.

Unfathomable is the length, breath and depths of our souls. How do you articulate such a miracle as this, for the image of God Himself is captured within. Our souls like our minds seem to have two distinct divisions. Our minds of course possess both a conscious and a subconscious level while our souls seem to have much the same capacity. We have a conscious level that contains all who we are on this earth. All the good points of ourselves and all the bad, all our knowledge and experiences all our longings and successes the best of us and the worst of us which make us into the person or personality we see today, the human and earthly side of us is contained in this more pervasive and aware side of our soul.

This more material side of ourselves of our soul, is the ever evolving side, hopefully ever growing side. This is your human one of a kind earthly individualization. No one is exactly quite like you. No one else has had the same childhood experiences as you, no one had your body, your mind, your mosaic of events that make you, you.

No two snowflakes, no two blades of grass, no two fingerprints, or irises are the same; and no two people are either. This side of your soul, this conscious stream of temperament, and deduction is sadly the side most people are quite familiar with. You have used this personality of yours to forge out a life for yourself, to integrate into society and to sail yourself on these waters of human existence ever caught up in the moment ever spinning in the wind.

We think this game of chasing and gathering is what life is all about but that is simply a childish and youthful view. The years will pile on the chasing will get more laborious and the gathering quite unfulfilling. There will always be a certain tugging at you, a silent prodding urging you to look deeper into yourself to reveal within the second part of your soul the higher; purer, unconscious qualities that you possess, and are the very image of God.

Let us make man in our image is that higher consciousness of peace, harmony, love, that very seed of God planted in you, in the fields of your soul. Your true self is that you are an individualization of God and with that realization your soul awakens. So the spiritual man, the Christ within, the divine mind, becomes self-conscious in you, and you will never be the same. It will find your true place in life and put you in it. It will inspire you with new thoughts new ideas. It will shape your life effortlessly once you unleash its power and set it to work in affairs. Now you have no limits no boundaries nothing to curb you as you rise higher and higher in consciousness.

Truth is truth, today, tomorrow and yesterday and the truth is God by placing Himself within man makes man part of His Divine Expression, His Divine scheme. When we feed or recognize this "seed of life" within our souls, God's presence, we enter into God's perfect plan. With one God, there can be only one plan, and we have been graciously invited to be a part. This recognition is the subjugation of your free will. It is you realizing that the best part of you isn't you at all, but the qualities of God placed within.

Less of me and more of you, (God) should be our desire. We live, move and have our being with God at the helm of our lives. The captain of our ship is the spiritual substance, your soul, which underlies and sustains every activity of mind and body.

To establish ourselves, to work with the spirit within is the true gateway of life. There is no other. God is the Father of our being, the director of life. Go deep down into your soul's center and give the Spirit an opportunity to reveal to you all the desires of your heart, all which is truly worthwhile. The Psalms say to "Delight thyself also in the Lord and He shall give you the desires of your heart". God gave us a soul so we may evolve to be like Him, the soul gives us one of the greatest characteristics we could possibly possess, the ability to communicate directly with the Almighty the ability to speak the language of God. The ability to pray and have two way communication with God Himself, to truly hear his voice and recognize it. There is no greater talent within than this!!!

Your Celestial Cell Phone

It was a hot and steamy mid-August day when I arrived back home from Pioneer Village. Pioneer Village was an awesome escape into the deep woods of western Massachusetts. Hiking, camping, swimming, Pioneer Village had it all, but even with all that distraction at hand, I couldn't wait to get back to my beloved Kawasaki KS 125 motorcycle. At 15 years of age this little machine was the highlight of my life. We've spent many an afternoon together and rode down many a trail to the point that I and my motorcycle had become one. Scarey.

It had been a whole week since I rode it, so even the fact of a little rain couldn't stop me from taking her out. I filled her with gas, kicked her over and off we went. I hit those trails pumped and was having the time of my life until an act of carelessness curbed everything. I was going 30 to 35 mph on a familiar trail when I came to a rock I traditionally would pull a wheelie over. I gassed it up and pulled on my handlebars to get lift, but this time it was different. My front tire just slid off the wet stone and pointed me to a stone wall. The acceleration pulled me back off the throttle and I lost all control. I hit the stone wall at about 30 mph, bad enough, but it was the oak tree behind it that did me in.

All I remember is waking up in the most intense pain I'd ever felt. I knew my leg was broken, I knew my wrist was broken, what I didn't know was that 3 ribs were cracked and I had a major concussion. I relate this story to you because it was one of the most helpless, pain full, and petrified times of my life to that point. I wasn't going to stand up and walk out of this, besides that fact it was 1974 and there was no such thing as a cell phone. I couldn't just reach into my coat, grab my IPhone, and give rescuers my satellite coordinates.

I laid there screaming at the top of my lungs but no one heard me. I was there for hours passing in and out of consciousness. I could see my bike about 50 feet away, it seemed like 50 miles but I finally reached it. Thankfully the horn was still working. I propped a stick up against the horn button and let her rip.

I remember praying, begging God for help and it's not like I was very spiritual back then I was 15. My neighbor walking his dog heard the horn and found me. I relay this story to you because it was one of the most vivid, painful, helpless and lonely moments I ever experienced. I was all alone, totally cut off, no one knew that I was in trouble and I was desperately scared out of my mind. There seemed nothing I could do.

Many of us feel this way today without running into a tree. We feel totally cut off and alone. No one can hear you and you need help now. It can be the everyday rigors of life that have you feeling this way or it could be tragic or traumatic occurrence in your life leaving you out of control.

In the case of my motorcycle accident had it been a few years later, technology would have saved me a whole lot a pain and worry. I could have called 911 and had an ambulance there inside of 10 minutes. What a secure feeling knowing I can reach out and get the help I need when I need it. Having that little insurance policy, that cell phone makes us all feel a little better it is technology that warms the heart.

We as humans as created beings in His image possess a technology far beyond what any cell phone could possibly do. We have at our disposal a celestial cell phone, a technology that can transport your consciousness directly into the presence of the Lord Himself. In the creating of us in His image and through the many complexities of the soul, we have a power within that many of us are simply not aware of. We just whip out our celestial cell phone power it up, and let it make our lives a little easier. It has many uses and an infinite amount of powerful apps.

The most important of these applications is of course the ability to communicate directly with the Creator. People think they know what prayer is, but sadly the majority does not. They intuitively know it's important, but do not have the discipline to follow thru and really try it out in the most practical of senses. Most people do not speak the language of God. In order to do so you must still the reasoning mind and give God the right of way. He speaks in a still small voice on His own frequency. We must learn to match up these frequencies and tap into His infinite power. Prayer is the realm of inspiration, the realm of illumination, and the realm of revelation.

It is attained with discipline for we must be willing to give of ourselves. As in any relationship it is a giving of ourselves, it is a back and forth dynamic, it is "He who dwelleth". There is nothing on this planet more valuable than a two way relationship with God acquired through prayer, nothing.

People will often ask the question why I must continually pray to God. He knows what I need, He knows what I want, why must I constantly ask Him over and over again. Is He forgetful, or just slow to get things done? No but prayer is a form of teamwork. It is you working in conjunction with God to get something done. We use prayer in an intelligent way to build the kind of life we want. We are like the architect drawing up plans of what is to be. Houses don't just magically appear on empty house lots now do they? They take much planning and preparation ahead of time. Prayer provides the subconscious and God with a blueprint of the work that is to be done. Diligent prayer will see it through. We build in thought and prayer the conditions that will manifest themselves on the physical plane. This takes teamwork. God does know our needs, our aspirations and dreams. Something within our souls desires a richer more complete life. Something in our innermost being knows that greater things lie ahead for us, endless possibility. We must not just wait around for things to just miraculously happen we in partnership with God must set things in motion we must remember, God is the creator but man is the builder.

We are capable of endless expansion and growth. It is the knowledge that our attitudes, our beliefs, our thoughts are what shape our destiny. When we focus on the greater good, when we align ourselves with the power of God within, we are more open to our true reality.

We pray every day, we pray with discipline because all of your old attitudes, all your opposing beliefs are altered only through persistent and conscious affirmation of new ones, new attitudes, new beliefs. We must refocus our attention and align ourselves with His wholeness, His power, His thinking. All this simply cannot be done by just going to church on Sunday or praying every once in a while if the mood strikes you.

Persistence is required for all this new thinking to become second nature. We must retrain our subconscious minds that have been filled with the world's teachings of limitation, lack, sickness and disease. We must have a subservient belief that if Jesus say's I'm capable of something then I'm capable. And just because it may not look like it right now we must believe it will in the end. Everything is a process. He who dwelleth in the secret place, he who spends time in prayer, is he who reaches God and abideth under the shadow (protection) of the Almighty.

When we tune ourselves to Him, when we give Him the time required in prayer and meditation wondrous and miraculous things occur. To be proficient at anything requires continual practice, athletes, musicians, teachers they all know there is no way around it. Why not be proficient at the most important and practical undertaking you could have in your life, prayer.

Listen if depression has a hold on you supplant it with right thinking, healthy thinking. You have holes in your life you want changed, couple with God in prayer and change them, sit in the very shadow of God and receive His protection. Retrain your conscious and subconscious mind with the power and word of the Creator Himself. This is not religious mumbo-jumbo it is the practical use of the gift of prayer we all possess. Drill these words into that concrete slab that we call our minds. Prayer really does change things and prayer only works in the proportion that we allow it. It pulls strings and influences things we would never be able to on our own. It's really not magic but it is magical in the sense of its results. Don't take my word for it or anyone's for that matter but give it a hard test for yourself, I promise you won't be disappointed.

God our heavenly Father is the Creator of the whole universe. It is perfect and self-fulfilling. We have been placed down here on this earth to be little creators. God created the whole universe but leads it up to us to create our own individualized world's or (lives). Like a chip off the old block we are always creating whether we realize it or not.

Matt 5; "Blessed are they which do hunger and thirst after righteousness (God) for they and (their lives) shall be filled". Make prayer time with God a habit that you cannot live without, make it the cornerstone of your life and your life will never be the same.

Spirituality is a step by step process which we allow ourselves to grow into. It doesn't happen all at once, it evolves bit by bit it matures piece by piece, moment by moment. It must be nourished along like the in-laws and the bank accounts. We must learn to endow everything we do with our Spirit, with our inner most being.

From the most trivial to the most traumatic we must incorporate a certain awareness about us that God is involved in every aspect of your life, big or small. In the seventeenth century a monk named Brother Lawrence wrote about this "heightened awareness of God". He called it Practicing the Presence of God. It sounds overwhelming but in reality it is very subtle, very peripheral.

This type of awareness is not offered up to just monks and mystics for the truth is it is designed for the everyday, normal hectic life. It is not brought about by chants or long hours spent meditating. Brother Lawrence described it as a, "simple attentiveness and a loving gaze upon God". He would later on describe it as a "habitual silent and secret conversation of the soul with God". We must always be aware and believe that our most personal issues of life are dear to the very Heart of the Lord.

It is an undercurrent of awareness of the Lord's presence in your life and it brings a sense of peace and direction in your everyday living. It is with you as you rush off to pick the kids up from school, it is with you when you wake up to start your day. It is with you throughout your crazy and hectic life and it is with you in the peace and silence of your alone time. It is with you always and your job is to bring it a little closer to the surface of your everyday routine.

Practical Christianity is for practical life, and to live without it is practically suicide. Listen you are very aware of your cell phone. We are at the point today that if we forget to take it with us, if we lose it, it is comparable to losing a limb. Many people experience high anxiety if their cell phone is not right next to them, fully charged. We should cultivate that same level of awareness when it comes to our soul, our celestial cell phone. Every day we should realize we have it and use it. Forgetting about it is worse than losing a limb because instead we can lose the life He has planned for us. Our celestial cell phones are priceless they come with unlimited range, unlimited minutes, there are no contracts or early termination fees, and the battery never dies out. Go out and try to find a better plan. You won't. In all seriousness let me ask you one question, are you more aware of your earthly cell phone than your heavenly one. Think about it. Prayer is so utterly fundamental yet so unsuspected by the world at large!!

King Me!!

Today we are going to look at one of the most perplexing questions that a sincere follower of God could ask. A question that many pastors and religious leaders today would rather stay away from and won't usually bring up unless cornered or forced into, often times with the cliché answers, it's a mystery, or that's just the way it is, or the most worn out one of all it's God's will. That question of questions is why do some people's prayers get answered and others don't. Why do some people heal and some don't. Why with two people diagnosed with the same sickness does one survive and one succumb?

Why does God answer some people's prayers and then seemingly ignore others. Does God play favorites, am I worthy? Is there a secret to all this prayer stuff? Do I have any control of this roller coaster life I'm living? Can I even have control? The answer is yes, yes, yes.

We need two tools to unlock this mystery, one the all-powerful word of God, (your Bible) and two the use of your spiritual eyes, not your material but your spiritual eyes. The Bible is the book of every man a manual of the soul's development and everything in it from Genesis to Revelation is really concerned with that unfolding, that is to say the spiritual awakening of the individual. You and your problems are analyzed from every possible angle and the fundamental lessons of spiritual truth are put forth in all sorts of different ways to meet every possible condition and every human need.

In the Bible sometimes we are fishermen, navigating the waters of life, sometimes we are shepherds tending our flocks, sometimes we are high priests or even a beggar. But it is as a King we will consider ourselves today. Today we are monarchs. Today we rule. So let us get in character and see what we can learn.

Each man or woman is the ruler of a kingdom although they know it not, and that kingdom is nothing less than the world of his own life and experience. The Bible is full of stories of Kings and their kingdoms, of wise kings that became foolish kings, of wicked kings and righteous kings, victorious kings and defeated kings and the rise and fall of their respected kingdoms.

When we are put into this context we discover the truth, that we are the absolute monarchs of our lives, not as a metaphor but as a literal fact. We build or destroy our own conditions in life. We can build or destroy our own health, our own finances and especially the climate of our lives. We attract to ourselves certain kinds of people, others we repel. We attract to ourselves riches or poverty, war or peace, slavery or freedom all in accordance with how we govern our kingdoms.

Now of course the world at large does not see it this way, the world feels that life is thrust upon them, that outer circumstance and people mold their general sphere of life. That happenstance and luck (good or bad) govern their world, and that they are just along for the ride. Nothing could be farther from the truth.

We are the monarchs of our own lives make no mistake about it. We rule our personal kingdoms today much the same way the great kings of the Bible did many centuries ago. When we realize, when we truly grasp the fact that the condition of one's life, one's kingdom, are not made up for him by outer circumstance or by other people, we realize that it is truly us ourselves that create our lives, this awareness becomes our ticket to true freedom and liberty. We approach life a little differently now.

Nothing but misfortune and confusion could possibly follow us if we base our lives on a false principle or promise, and this is what has happened to many a man or woman and their respected kingdoms. Listen we all get curveballs in life, unexplainable tragedies, unwanted sorrows, but it's your life's general overall cadence that counts. When the dust has settled, and everything has panned out, you'll have had the important things in life, the things that were meant for you and for you alone. Emerson states; "The things that are really for thee gravitate to thee. A man cannot escape from his good. A man is sure that his welfare is dear to the heart of the Lord". We have been deceived about the nature of life and ourselves, and that is why Jesus "Savior of the World" said, "Know the truth and the truth shall make you free". That is why He spent His years of public life in teachings and explaining the Truth, telling us about the nature of God and man, and how to live life abundantly.

As Christians and kings we were commanded by Jesus our true King to seek first the kingdom of God and all His righteousness. Then when asked, well where is this kingdom where can it be found? Jesus replied, "The Kingdom of God is within you". Forever laying to rest the notion that God is distant, aloof or far off. He is actually closer than our own breath, closer than hands and feet. Listen being made in His image in His likeness, places the kingdom of God within your very own soul, and heaven itself within your very grasp. Without your soul we humans are just the backdrop of nature no higher than the animal kingdom, but with it (soul) we can command the world and gravitate toward God. Your soul is your Holy Grail.

When a king got confused or had an important decision to make he would seek council often returning into a special room or chamber. They would call this chamber, the war room or council chamber or the secret chamber for whatever was said there stayed there. The king would privately meet there with his generals and confidants to discuss strategy or whatever weighed on his mind before making any big decisions. The people in that room knew that their very lives depended on their confidentiality and trust. No one dares breach that trust.

As rulers of our own individual kingdoms we have been given much the same place to meet with our heavenly council, a private chamber where we can openly reveal ourselves, our fears, our wants, we can cry out to God knowing no one else can hear us, we are safe, and we can receive wise and Godly council from the King of Kings and Lord of Lords Himself. There we can know our prayers are being heard. There we know for certain we have the very ear of God. There is where our true power lies.

This room, this chamber is called in the Bible, (King James) (Psalm 91) The Secret Place of the most High and there we find sanctuary. Psalm 91). "He that dwelleth in the Secret Place of the Most High, abideth under the shadow of the Almighty. I will say of the Lord He is my refuge and my fortress, my God in Him shall I trust". In life if you are ever too troubled or too scared to pray when you can't even seem to think straight, or situations are overpowering you, use these powerful words as your own. Say them with conviction and meaning, and confirm the truth they contain, then these words shall never fail you.

Verse 15 reads; "He (you) shall call upon me, and I will answer him. I will be with you in times of trouble I will deliver you, and honor you". God does not make promises He doesn't intend to keep. There has never been a wasted or idle word from the mouth God.

The Secret Place of the Most High is your own mind or consciousness. This is one of the most practical important discoveries you could ever make for yourself. The error that most people usually fall into is to assume that the Secret Place of the Most High is somewhere outside themselves some far off distant place up in the sky. But Jesus says no that the kingdom of God is within you and that the kingdom of God is at hand.

We need look no further for God than our own minds and prayers. We have been given the opportunity to climb right inside our own mind our own stream of thought and commune directly with the Divine. We leave behind the realm of the physical and all its material senses to enter into the realm of the spiritual, God's realm. In God's realm thought is the mode of communication and to mentally dwell with the Almighty, to dwelleth in the secret place, is simply giving God your undivided attention. We close out the world of haste and worry and give oneself totally over to Him. To enter into ones prayer closet is to enter into one's own mind, your own consciousness, your own secret place.

We say to God you are worthy of my time and you have all of me and all of my attention. This is not a one time in and out office visit with the doctor for the Psalm states that it is he that "dwelleth" in the Secret Place" that it is he who visits frequently and stays awhile is promised the protection and provision of the Almighty. This man or woman will abideth under the shadow of the Almighty under His protection. As the great and majestic bald eagle spreads her wings and covers her little eaglets in times of duress so does our Lord open up his everlasting arms and pulls us close enough to be in His very shadow his very bosom in time of need.

This leads me back into the question we asked earlier. Why don't my prayers get answered? Why does God feel so distant? Why can't I hear from Him? Listen if we ever had a top ten list for scripture memorizing Psalm 91 is one to be downloaded for this one teaching when correctly understood can truly revitalize your life and put you on a road of spiritual wholeness and oneness. Open those rusty gates of your consciousness and allow the Spirit of life to flow through, turn sorrow into joy and sadness into song.

Once you have experienced Jesus in the light of this teaching you will never be the same again. Psalm 91; "He who dwelleth in the Secret Place off the Most High will abideth under the shadow of the Almighty". This entire psalm is a spiritual treatment powerful words being put in our mouths by God Himself. The rest of it underpins the first statement, it is just a literary marvel the way it lays to rest fear and anxiety. It reaches right into the human psyche like no secular psychology ever could for it doesn't just treat the mind but reaches right into your very soul.

It knows you. It knows you better than you know yourself, and has helped countless millions of people. People who have learned to go to the Psalms for healing. God's word knows no bounds, knows no wound it can't heal, or ache it can't quench. Every need there has ever been is covered in the Bible, every answer is there. We must seek, we must find, we must make contact, real contact.

This way of thinking, that God is distant, or outside of you is fatal to our hopes and dreams because our prospects of success in prayer depend upon our succeeding in getting some degree of contact with God. He is to be contacted from within and not from without. Abundant life comes from within not from without.

To make contact spiritually we must close off the material world, shutting everything out is imperative. Yes we can pray to God in a busy bus station, in our cars, wherever, but if we are looking for a miracle, seeking His strength, reaching out, then I'm going to my prayer closet, which is really my mind, my sanctuary, my secret place.

Giving God my undivided attention while I'm driving down the highway is not what I would call quality time. Getting alone getting quiet and reaching that secret place of the Most High is reiterated by Jesus when He called out the Pharisee's for praying in the streets, out in the open. Matt; (6-5) "And when thou prayest, thou shall not be as the hypocrites are; for they love to pray standing in the synagogues and in the corners of the streets, that they may be seen of men. Verily I say unto you they have their reward. But when thou prayest enter into thy closet (mind) and when thou has shut the door pray to thy Father which is in secret; and thy Father which seeth in secret shall reward thee openly". Jesus called it the prayer closet and in that closet or quiet space we bring about something akin to a miracle. Morgan Freeman narrates a new series on the science channel called; Through the Worm Hole. In a segment on human consciousness they describe human thought or prayers as "conscious projections of energy" that can "reach out beyond the physical and into the very cosmos itself". It's a force it's not hocus pocus, it's the real deal even if we can't fully grasp the complexities of it at our present level of understanding. Prayer is a conscious projection of thought and energy. A projection that invariably hits it's target and makes contact.

We make contact, contact with that still small voice. To have the effectual prayer of a righteous man we must make a connection, we must make intimate contact with our Lord. We must really want to seek God on this level. We must develop a love for this type of intimacy.

Who Touched Me?

Imagine if you were one of those few lucky people who experienced Jesus physically back in the first century, to be able to look in those eyes or hear that voice. What would you do what would you say? You do know that you can speak to Jesus just as John did, just as Peter and James and all the apostles did. You can receive from Him a miracle just as the blind man or the leper or anyone else who was lucky enough to cross His path in that day. I mean real contact with Him just as the woman at the well or the woman who reached out to touch the hem of His garment. Instead of using your hands today to reach out we use a different part of our bodies, we use our minds in prayer. With our mind we can touch the hem of His garment. Let us look at this teaching we find in (Matt 9) of a woman who made real contact with our Lord and it changed her life forever.

(Mark 5-21) We are given a place (the secret place) where we know we can find the very presence of our Lord we can reach out to Him and touch Him just as this poor ailing woman did two thousand years ago. We must have that one quality that she possessed that one trait that makes all the difference a special attribute that many of us don't have. The missing ingredient that opens the door to any miracle we might seek, that one requirement that keeps many a sincere Christian from total victory is a pure and dynamic childlike belief. To combine real contact with real belief is absolute dynamite for the soul. With the faith the size of a mustard seed we can move a mountain and don't let anyone ever tell you any different.

Pure belief allows the believer to draw on God's power and strength, it is a natural byproduct of an abiding relationship (dwelleth with) with God. In this instance (Mark 5-25) Jesus was voluntarily giving of Himself to heal the masses He was on his way to Jairus's home to look at his sick little girl. Word had gotten out that Jesus was there and the people came out of the woodwork. Before they knew it He was mobbed and it was bedlam. (Mark 25) "And a certain woman which had an issue of blood for twelve years, and had suffered many things of many physicians, and had spent all that she had, and was nothing better but rather grew worse". Because of the frenzy this woman could not get close enough to Jesus to ask Him for a healing she could not look into his face and plead with him like all the others. She could not physically speak to him because she was being physically overpowered by the throng. (Mark 27) "When she had heard of Jesus she came in the press from behind, and touched his garment. For she said if I may touch but his clothes, I shall be whole. And straightway the fountain of her blood was dried up; and she felt in her body that she was healed of that plague". This tortured soul was able, by her simple childlike faith to draw the power of a healing from Jesus without physically asking Jesus for it. She was miraculously and completely healed without Jesus actually consenting, facing or touching her. That's important to note for she took the responsibility of healing herself, she reached out to Jesus and she initiated the whole process. She decided to take step one, she reached out. Isn't that what we all do when we pray? Well then why did she get such outstanding results.

Line 28 in Mark tells us "because she thought" in her mind she knew, if I just touch His clothes I will be healed. She simply knew that it would happen and nothing was going to stop her. Her childlike belief was operating on a higher level than the average person and it wasn't and I repeat wasn't because she physically reached out and touched His garment with her hand. It was because she spiritually reached out with her mind that was bent on belief and made contact with Him. Jesus did not initiate this healing she did. She reached out she took initiative and responsibility proving we can too.

This is proved by Jesus's response. He did feel her little tug of His hem, but that is not what got His attention, for He was being mauled by the throng. No He felt something much different, He felt power had gone out of Him or stated elsewhere loss of virtue. That stopped Him dead in His tracks to ask the question who touched me? He seemed astonished to know that there was someone in the crowd with that type of faith. The apostles not knowing what was going on said to Him, are you kidding. Who touched you? You see all these people crowding you and you ask who touched you? But Jesus persisted knowing the tremendous example this woman would be for generations to come. Jesus asks again, who touched me? In fear and trembling the woman admitted it was her, and in love and compassion Jesus responded "daughter your faith has healed you, go in peace free from your suffering".

In our Secret Place of the Most High, in our prayer closets we can make contact much the same way as she did. Possessing a mustard seed of faith we can make Jesus stop dead in His tracks and ask, who touched me? What unbridled joy it would be for the initiator in prayer to cry out, "It was I Lord". "It was I that touched you" and then to be comforted by the words of the Lord, well then, go in peace and suffer no more.

It's in how we approach Him. It's that mustard seed of faith that childlike belief that initiates contact and makes Jesus ask who touched me? We don't need to beg God for answered prayer, we don't grovel before Him and try to rationalize whether we are worthy or not, if we deserve it? We stand on our two feet and know the truth. It is God's great joy in answering prayer and giving us all good things, he takes great pleasure in giving us the keys to the kingdom.

Let's break this down to its most elemental form. What parent out there if asked by his or her (little pumpkin) for a present at Christmas time, a present that was good and easily available to you, what parent wouldn't go out of his way and get it, and then what parent wouldn't derive as much joy as the child when they see their "little pumpkin" explode with excitement at his or her new toy. It is His great joy to give us the keys to the kingdom, for our joy is his joy.

Jesus stopped everything He was doing to point out that woman's faith. To make an example of her, and her unshakeable belief that Jesus could heal her. Out of the multitudes of people that were groping and reaching out for Christ that day Jesus stopped and put her on a pedestal for all to see lifting up her faith for generations to come. Often times when Jesus wants to drive home a certain point or teaching He will reiterate that point again almost immediately as He does here when He continues to Jairus's house. Jairus was a ruler of the synagogue and his daughter was dying. Again what parent wouldn't do anything including trading places to save the life of the child they love so much.

Even to approach Jesus was a great risk to Jairus. His job, his social standing, everything he stood for at that point in his life was at stake, but he didn't care. He was desperate and found no hope in his religious system, so he fell at the feet of Jesus and pleaded with Him. On their way to the house they were told it's too late your daughter has died. Ignoring them Jesus said "don't be afraid and just believe".

When they arrived the people were crying and wailing loudly. Jesus asked why all the commotion and wailing, the child is not dead, just asleep. Take notice of the people's reaction to that statement. They laughed at Him. Isn't that what the world does today? When we speak of these things we get ridiculed by proposing that all things are possible for those who know Christ. The funny thing is it's usually the religious leaders and people in authority that laugh the loudest and doubt the most.

So what should we do? We do what Jesus did. He cleared that house of unbelief. He put them all out, just as we need to clear out our own houses, our own minds, our own lives of the plague we call unbelief. Before we can fully participate in all the graces of God we must cleanse ourselves of doubt, fear and uncertainty and replace it with Jesus's own words, don't be afraid, suffer no more, and just believe.

It doesn't matter one bit whether you are young or old, Jesus was twelve when He astounded the priest of the temple and Nicodemus was an old man when Jesus opened his eyes and he became a born again child of God.

Today let us rule our kingdom hand in hand with the King of Kings let us be the monarch of our lives rather than slaves to it. Let us lean on the promises of God with renewed vigor and aggressiveness and give life back a little taste of its own medicine. Who touched me, Jesus asked? I hope for our sakes it is us, that we are the ones reaching out to make real contact and live the divine life that was meant for us today. I hope for our sakes it is us so that we may fire on all cylinders.

Jesus said all the power is given unto me to bring heaven upon this earth. If our lives resemble hell more than heaven then we must ask ourselves some hard questions of our relationship with Christ and what we really believe and not just profess, for if unto us is given His Power how then can we fail?

Personal Responsibility

I don't believe that Jesus showed us His ability to heal, His oneness with the Father, His incredible miracles so that out of the masses of people a few so called faith healers or miracle workers such as Benny Hinn could arise. We need to take personal responsibility for the condition of our body, mind and soul. We possess inside of us the Christ Consciousness which will guide each one of us in all our paths. Each of us must take the initiative to develop this power within us.

Make no mistake about this, we all have it. It is not a gift given to just a chosen few.

I think sometimes Jesus just made it too simple, too easy for a people that have become used to suffering and pain. Swimming upstream all the time takes great energy, believing on the promises of God takes none. Just believe and go with the flow. With that Jesus walked to that little girl and said, I say to you, get up, and immediately she rose proving life and death are at the very feet of Jesus. Prove all this for yourself, touch the hem of his garment, answer Him when He asks "who touched me", and thank Him when He says "suffer no more".

The Perfect Side Of Your Soul

Roman 7, 15-25

(15) "For that which I do I allow not (disapprove) For what I would, (approve of) that do I not. But what I hate, that I do. (19) For the good that I would, I do not but the evil which I would not, that I do. (20) Now if I do that, I would not, it is not I that do it but sin that dwelleth in me. (21) I find then a law, that when I would do good, evil is present with me. (23) But I see another law in my members, warning against the law of my mind, and bringing me into captivity to the law of sin which is in my members. (24) O wretched man that I am who shall deliver me from the body of this death. (25) I thank God through Jesus Christ our Lord, So then with the mind I serve the law of God; but with the flesh the law of sin".

Now that is what I call a conflicted man. Paul sounds as if he doesn't know if he is coming or going. He seems a little ashamed of himself and rather perplexed at his behavior. All the things he should do he doesn't and all the things he shouldn't be doing he does. Does this game of spiritual tug of war sound familiar? How comforting is it to know that one of the greatest spiritual giants of our time, Paul himself suffered from all the same failures we face today, that the imperfect side of ourselves would triumph so often over the perfect side of our souls.

I absolutely love Paul's brutal assessment of himself. He doesn't try to (pretty up) himself or make excuses, he just lays it out bare. No make-up no floss. This ongoing battle this inner conflict is further testament to the uniqueness of your soul. This clash going on inside isn't between two opposing countries, or groups of people, this is between you and you.

Can you imagine the United States launching a nuclear attack on Washington, or Russian soldiers fighting Russian soldiers within its own borders? It sounds ridiculous but your soul does put you in that ominous position never the less. For contained within your soul is the (seed of perfection). A white hot spark from a white hot flame, perpetually burning itself into your members as Paul would put it. Paul later says in Romans; 8-23, we groan within ourselves, waiting for the adoption to wit (happen) the redemption of our body.

That is exactly what God did. God adopted the human race and redeemed mankind. He opened His heart and allowed us into His family, His world, His reality, knowing inside how much good He could do us, how much better off we would be with His help and guidance and love. He knew it wouldn't be easy, He knew it would take time but He was willing to make that kind of investment which says to me in His eyes we are worth it.

So the soul itself becomes a battlefield with two combatants ever contending for supremacy of the heart. There is self (you) and there is truth (God's soul) locked horn in horn like two rams forever pulling, forever pushing, forever snorting in disgust. Truth is the only reality in the world. It is not hidden it is not deviated. It is always available, always revealed and perfectly transparent. It is inward harmony, perfect love, equality of justice. It seems we have two masters within and Jesus said "No man can serve two masters, for either he will hate the one and love the other or he will hold to the one and despise the other".

Jesus conquered His human nature. Jesus learned to deny His self and looked inward for His Source. He kindled the spark of perfection and fanned it into a great flame. Jesus knew that self is sneaky and subtle and vain and that truth is simple and uncompromising. Jesus gave all the credit to that (seed of perfection within) when He said to the Pharisees, "It is not I that do these great works or miracles but it is the Father within me". "I can do nothing of myself but for the Father". "These words are not my words but come from the Father". That same seed of perfection that Jesus found is planted within you. Jesus rested within the Father and so can you. No fear, no doubt, no anxiety, marred his expression, "Let not your heart (mind) be troubled" said Jesus "for I'am with you even to the end of the world". Let me ask you if the Lord is with us, whom then shall we fear?

Jesus was able to do all the great works He did because He attained victory over Himself that Paul found so infuriating. This battle within our very souls is as frustrating and humbling as it gets, but it proves humanities special uniqueness toward God, his oneness. Now where else in nature does this inner conflict exist? Does the lion lament over killing the elk? Does the elephant have guilt pangs over harsh words with the monkey? Does the seagull lose sleep for crapping all over your car in the supermarket parking lot? I think not.

God making man in His image placing within us a piece of Himself, acquiring the knowledge of good and evil, preps the way for our dual personalities. Our souls are our moral compasses that lift us out of the animal kingdom that surrounds us. How far it lifts us out is totally up to us. It's hard to chart how far we've come because we still have so far to go. The future holds endless opportunity for us when we have learned to listen to that perfect side of our souls. The promises of God can all be fulfilled in us, if we are faithful to the truth.

To master the self-side of our souls is to attain dominion over the mind. Poise, self-control is the gateway to perfect peace and abundance. It gives one a true and authoritative expression of wisdom and understanding. It is the perfect side of the soul that teaches us the way of life, of peace and power and prosperity. The perfect side of the soul makes us both saint and sinner. It is all in how we deal with this schizophrenic dance that determines the outcome good or bad for this earthly life lesson we all share in.

God has a purpose for you. He has a work for you to do and that "perfect side of your soul" that Godly seed will tell you when, where, and how as soon as you are ready to listen and obey. "Be ye therefore perfect even as your Father which is in heaven is perfect". Jesus in this instance was admonishing the people to display a "perfect love" a love that does not come naturally to man, telling us to keep with it, to work it, to mold it, over and over till we get it right. He knew we were a long way off but He also knew that a seed of perfection had been planted, and He knew roots would soon take hold. He knew within us was a piece of the Father and He knew because of that our potential was endless. Jesus had to have had the patience of a saint in dealing with the people of his time.

This perfect side of our being is our higher self it is the piece of us that is touched by God. It has perfect understanding and is perfect truth. The same hand that holds the entire universe together holds your hand too. It never fails or falters, it is never confused and it can't be shaken. It boldly says, "I will arise and go to my Father". I will establish within me my true self and fulfill my true destiny. I will no longer give into selfishness. I will no longer contaminate my mind with miss-truths and hatred which robs me of my true inheritance. I will start a raging fire with the spark of the Lord inside me and with it warm all those around me. Its light shall be so bright that no one can resist its brilliance. Like moths to a flame and it will lead many a dark and fear laden soul to its sanctuary and protection. They shall abide under the shadow of the Almighty.

I will say just what Jesus said to all those who see the miraculous change in me. It is not me that does these things, but the Father within me. I can do nothing but in conjunction with the "perfect side of my soul" all things are possible for those who know and love God. We chase after so much in life, love, health, money, all those things are like a butterfly seemingly always just outside of our grasp, till we give up sit down quietly and then let that elusive butterfly land on us of its own free will. It chooses us just as God chose us. His Spirit is diffused throughout all of humanity. We must uncover and reveal that which is already present at the center of our being, that perfect side of our soul. We must unify ourselves with the Divine Presence to discover who we really are. Once we do our path will be revealed and our footstep will be directed by God Himself. Once we do, we will for the first time, FIRE ON ALL CYLINDERS.

Flesh On The Bone

Many years ago just before I was about to deliver a sermon before a small group of people a well-respected friend of mine came up to me and said, "David when you go up there make sure you put some Flesh on the bone", he continued on to say to me," you must make it real for the people, make it personal or it's just words that never find their home". I stood there for a moment letting the words sink in when I realized he was right. I had sat through hundreds of sermons by many various pastors and preachers that seemed somehow hollow, or sterile. I can usually tell within the first few minutes if a person's heart and soul is in it, if he actually believes the words he is preaching or if he learned the lesson himself second hand. The old adage, "You have got to pay your dues if you want to sing the blues" is nothing to sneeze at. There is a particular stamp of authority on a person if he actually walked the walk and talked the talk, and most often you can tell if a person's life experience matches up with what they are trying to teach you. When they do line up there is a certain validity in their words that your soul recognizes, a truth has then registered in your head and that person has just put Flesh on the bone and you see it for what it is. Truth! It will last with you, it sticks in your head and you can't get rid of it or just turn it off. Truth has now done what truth is supposed to do it has made an indelible impact. You have actually really learned something and that is priceless. It is rare to come across that type of genuineness but when you do, take advantage sit and absorb. Truth is I have gone back and forth many times with myself on whether to include this section in the book. Often times putting Flesh on the bone is not so easy for the person doing it. It's not so easy for me, I much rather the anonymity of a computer key board or notebook, but if I were you I would be asking the question what gives this man (me) the authority to speak so boldly. What is his story which allows him to tell me anything worth listening to. Has he sung the blues? Has he paid his dues? Is he book learned or has he experienced the things he speaks of. If you the reader are reading these words then I the writer have decided to include this most personal section in my book. It wasn't an easy decision but all I ask is please be gentle with me!!!

I was born in New England on Feb. 26, 1960. My childhood was dominated by a hard core alcoholic father who proceeded to torture our family on a regular basis till his death in 1972. Life for me began at twelve years of age. I didn't know what I wanted to do at that early age but I did know what I didn't want to do and that was drink. My father taught me one important thing in life and that was never to be like him, never to allow something so destructive, to so dominate my life that I become a danger to all those around me. Maybe the fact of never having a real earthly father has made my searching for a heavenly one such a strong focus of my life. I have always intuitively looked toward God for my inspiration, guidance and love, and God has always answered my call. (He is my Father) I am college educated but philosophy and theology were never my majors. Most of my life's education came from the University of Parcel Service (U.P.S.) where I have put in 50 hour work weeks for over 30 years. I know these two career choices don't mix but it is what it is. I have owned homes, raised a family, I have loved and lost, loved and won. I have no Pulitzer Prizes or big book deals. I do most of my writing while on vacations or day's off. I have served in many different churches in many different roles over the years. I have been an elder, worship leader, evangelist and assistant pastor. I delight myself in the Lord and His law and have been a diligent seeker my whole life. I believe we must always grow and to break the chains of stagnation in our spiritual lives and to use God and His words in the most practical everyday sense.

I was around 15 years old when the movie the Exorcist came out. I wasn't aware it was playing when my friends and I decided to go catch a flick on a Friday night. We had no idea what we were getting into when we bought tickets for a different movie (it was rated R) and slipped into the "forbidden theatre". I had known fear before but this fear was different. This fear affected my soul. When I finally walked out of that theatre that night my safe little world had changed. I saw demons around every corner. I had bad dreams and lost sleep and that fear affected me (as a young teenager) profoundly. I did finally grow up and rationalized everything (of course) but it did show me how fear can be quite the motivator. I know after that movie it was God I wanted to be in tight with. You can have Satan with his bad breath and pea soup, I'm all set. It really saddens me as a human being to know that we seem to grow best under adversity that we can't just learn something for knowledge sake, it has to be delivered with a punch or we don't listen. If that is what it takes, that's what it takes and we continue to learn in pain. Years went by and the influence of that movie slowly dissipated but that fear I'll never forget.

I remember my wife calling me at work and telling me the doctor wants to see me. I had an annual D.O.T. physical a week or so back for work and trace elements of blood were found in my urine. I was told to tell my primary care physician and make an appointment. They drew blood and this must be the results of the blood work. I asked my wife to get the results from the doctor but the doctor wouldn't give her them. She wanted to see me face to face and wanted the appointment set up quickly. Ok so that was a little unnerving a little inconvenient but I went in to see her a few days later. My doctor's name was Dr. Agarwal and she was a young doctor, very upbeat and positive, so her serious expression threw me a little at first. She sat me down looked me right in the eyes and said I have some very disturbing news for you. Your blood tests came back revealing that you are infected with the Hepatitis C virus. She went on to explain that it is a blood born pathogen that can really wreak havoc with your liver and your life. The virus works very slow and can take decades to do its damage, but because of my numbers, (viral Load) she estimated that I've had it in my system for quite some time. I knew I hadn't been "quite myself" for a while but many of the symptoms simply mimic aging, chronic fatigue, headaches, fevers, fogginess. When I left the doctor's office that afternoon I was dazed and confused. How did I get it? I thought only intravenous drug users got it. I did my share of partying when I was young, but I would never touch a needle. This just can't be. I sat in my car going over what she said, my mind was numb and then life played one of those cruel jokes on me that seem to happen from time to time. As I was pulling out of my parking spot I noticed the license plate of the car directly in front of me, it was a vanity plate from the movie Back to the Future, written in bold black type were the words You're out of Time, that was my exclamation point for the day. I left that parking lot that day never to be the same. Fear was now sitting right next to me again, getting comfortable, spinning its ugly head around in circles and ready to stay awhile. My doctor scheduled me to have a liver biopsy right away and I remember sitting in the hospital in shock. How do you go from perfectly all right one moment to being acutely sick the next. You want to talk fear there are no words for this type of fear. It's very personal, very overwhelming. As I sat on that gurney waiting for my surgery I thought back to that movie I saw so long ago, the fear that was placed in me and how that fear of the devil drew me closer to God. Now I was about to face the ultimate fear, the loss of my life and life again would never be the same.

My prognosis turned out to be pretty dim. My viral count was off the charts, the liver biopsy showed I had moderate to severe scarring on my liver and that is not good considering the next step would be cirrhosis and then liver cancer. I needed to stop and reverse this situation right away or I would not be walking this earth in this body much longer. I was immediately scheduled to start treatment. Treatment consists of injecting yourself with a combination of drugs called Interferon and Ribavirin. This combo is injected twice a week for up to 12 months. I was told that it would make me pretty sick but nothing prepared me for the way my body reacted to these drugs. It made me feel as though a freight train was running through my head. Incredible fevers and headaches followed by cold chills and body aches. It makes your body sick enough to kill the virus but not quite sick enough to kill you. How nice. I had taken a few weeks off of work to adjust to my new routine but after just 1 week I knew I would never be able to do my physical work at UPS and remain in treatment. I was placed between a rock and a hard place. I simply could not afford to take a year off of work. I was not financially ready for this, and at that point in time the cure rate was only at 40%. I could stay on treatment for an entire year and still not be cured. I was at a loss and really did not know what to do. Again it saddens me that people including myself must be put in this type of situation before they turn whole heartedly to God for help, until we surrender completely to Him. We exhaust all avenues, we do all we can do on a human basis, we hit road block after road block till we reach our wits end and in total desperation as a last resort reach out to Him. These were my cold hard choices do I stay on treatment and hope for a cure or do I continue to work and feed my family. I did not have the flexibility financially to take 2 weeks off of work without pay never mind an entire year, but if I didn't do something I could be dead inside of 2 to 3 years. This situation I would not wish on my worst enemy if I had one, but then again.

Appreciation

We as busy human beings never really seem to appreciate things until they are threatened or gone. We get so captivated with everyday living, the grind, the struggle, the persevering that we regretfully take most things in our lives for granted. We never stop to smell the roses or to take in the more subtle things in life and then only after they are wretched away from us do we feel the sting. Once gone never to return, the ache begins, the hole is created and a piece of ourselves feels missing. We mourn, we hurt, we cry and we say to ourselves only if I had known this would happen I would have done things different. I would have told that person how much I loved them I would have started that exercise program. I would have put more quality time into my work into my family. We take our health for granted. We take people for granted, we take sunny days for granted and our sense of appreciation is lost on the everyday, routine of things. None of us can peer into tomorrow none of us can see what the future holds for us if we could we would learn how to appreciate the things that we have been blessed with. If we knew for sure, ahead of time, we would be losing a loved one what a tremendous impact that would have on that relationship. We would make every moment count every word would have meaning, every moment we would value more than gold. Time becomes the most precious of commodities. This is where I am coming from as I write these pages for I was given a glimpse of my future. I was given a prophetic message by a doctor some years back stating that I would not be around on this physical plane much longer. I was given a prognosis that I wouldn't wish upon anyone. I was given a mandatory death sentence that changed my life forever, and taught me the true art of appreciation. It was the genesis of this book and the impetus of the closest walk with God that I could allow myself on this physical plane. When you are told you are about to lose everything you want it all the more. Everything becomes ultra-precious and your appreciation of things goes through the roof. You now possess a new and profound eyesight, one you did not have before. Nothing is ordinary anymore, nothing. It is truly sad that it takes this type of jolt on your life to wake you up to living. In our youth we appreciate very little because we have all the time in the world or so we think. Days give way to years and years give way to middle age yet we still slumber to comatose at all the wondrous things around us, the simple things and the quiet times. Many of us unlucky ones have our lives torn away from us in car accidents and heart attacks never receiving that wakeup call never emerging from our lethargic slumber. Life and all its intricate beauty just passes us by like dust in the wind. It really shouldn't take a death sentence to wake us up to life, but more often than not it does. I was skating along thru life just like most of you are doing right now, this moment. I thought everything was o.k. for the most part. I didn't lack any of the necessities, I had a roof over my head, decent job, plenty of food and drink, loved ones and companions. I was lulled into a certain type of complacency and routine that kept my eyes only half open. My doctor became my alarm clock and when she went off with the news that my death was approaching my doorstep, I lurched from my sleep like a bucket of cold water had been poured on my head. I was fully awake now. I was listening intently now. I was seeing deeper now. I appreciated everything now, and at this predawn hour of my death I was for the first time in my life fully alive now.

I remember life back then as being sort of hazy and cut off. I was in a continual state of shock, numb and terribly confused. I have vague memories of dramatic pleadings with God in my prayers. Lord why me? I'm only in my forties. I have so much to still accomplish. Lord I served you and served you my whole life and this is what I get. If I die my whole family is in limbo is that what you want? I was angry really angry at God. This religious and spiritual stuff is all garbage. Thoughts of all the sick people I counseled thru the years throwing scripture at them like a doctor throwing pills, pleading with them to believe and to pray for the Lord to heal them, assuring them that He can. Philippians (4:13) Exodus (15-26) Psalm (103-3) (Luke 4:40) (Luke 5:13)

All of this reverberating in the back of my mind, but directed at me now. It's easy to be strong, cock sure of what you're saying and professing when you're not the one who's sick, when you're not the one who is being prayed for. Well guess what Davey you are the one who is sick, you are the one being prayed for and these verses at the time seemed like empty shell casing without any gun powder.

I am well aware of the stages one goes through when dealing with serious illness, first the denial, then the anger and ultimately the acceptance. I had seen the Lord do many miraculous things in people's lives. I have seen bodies healed and diseases eradicated but I've also seen death and the inevitable succumbing to it. It unnerved me to see that it seemed more like a crap shoot than a tangible course of action. Why does God heal one person but yet allows another to die. This question seared into my brain. I had no answers but lo and behold I was about to find out.

All Of This

The Lord put me in a situation where I had only two options. One was to allow myself to surrender to the fear, to the anger, to be mad at God for this seething injustice served upon me. That is the easy route that is our natural inclination. The other was to take a stand and fight. My whole life I had professed God's word to other people, inspiring other people, leading others to a realization of God and all the wonders He can do in one's life. To live as if God were really real to me and to stand on His word. Well guess what now it is my turn. My turn to stand on His word my turn to use this inner strength we've been given to use this power in the most practical sense, basically to save my life. I do believe that we all have an appointed time to die, and that appointment we can't miss no matter how bad we would want to. But on the flip side I see the majority of people cutting their lives short with extremely unhealthy life styles, minds that are plagued with sick thoughts and a weak relationship at best with the Creator who made you. This whole book is dedicated to the quest to fire on all cylinders. It is the implementation of preventative maintenance that will keep you from such a day as I have visited. Treat your body as the spiritual temple it is, exercise, eat balanced, and get the proper rest. Fill your mind with positive things, "As a man thinketh so he is", is a spiritual law when misdirected will have dire consequences in your life, but most importantly it is to develop a two way, vital and stimulating relationship with God. Know the word and the power there of for without it you are a drifting ship without an anchor. All of this I have known for a good part of my life, all of this I have stood forth and preached to all sorts of people from all walks of life and all of this knowledge was about to be put to the ultimate test in a fight not for someone else's life but for my own.

The Journey

Many a man or woman has made the false assumption that it is impossible to harmonize the teachings of the Bible, in respect to physical healing with that of modern science and medicine. We absolutely must not abandon the healing aspect of religion and God to the institution of modern science and medicine. The most sensible and effective method for healing is to utilize the skills and methods of both modern medicine and science with those of spiritual healings and wisdom. What we call common sense is itself an expression of Divine Wisdom, wise action must be added to our prayers and supplications. When God said, "Let us make man in our image He placed within us His Spirit and His intelligence. It is this intelligence that allows for all these breakthroughs in modern medicine. Louise Pasteur may not give God the credit for his advances in bacteriology but God doesn't need the credit. Penicillin doesn't need God's name next to it in the dictionary for it to work, it just does. God is the Great Physician illuminating man's mind, shining light into the dark recesses of sickness and disease. Most of modern medicine remains arrogant and stoic in its attitude toward God and spiritual healing, but that is o.k. as long as we know who to give the credit too. Dr. Jesus was the ultimate healer, He is still the same yesterday, and today and forever Heb. 13:8 and that is the hook I'm hanging my hat on. That is the intelligent choice. The use of everything that is available to you is of course the wisest course of action. Going to God whole heartedly should be your first step but certainly not your only one.

At this point my only two choices were pretty clear. I could go on Interferon and Ribavirin treatment for a year, become financially bankrupt and hope I fall into the 40% of people that clear the virus from their system or take God at His word, surrender my heart, and take action through spiritual science and healing. I studied all about Hepatitis C. I looked at all the homeopathic therapies and treatments. I began a regiment that included all three cylinders in this human existence.

For my body I took a combination of herbs that have proven themselves down through the centuries to aid in the healing of liver ailments Milk Thistle, Silymarin, Licorice root, Dandelion root and a multi vitamin. I improved my diet to include fresh vegetables and whole foods. I changed some lifelong bad habits and started getting the proper sleep and rest I needed. I for the first time started treating my body like the precious jewel it is, and believe me it responded.

For my mind. I did the best I could to cleanse my mind of all fear. All thoughts of death and dying I replaced with affirmation of truths. My body is a spiritual temple indwelled by the very spirit of God, it is perfect, it is healthy, it is clean. My blood is as pure as a fresh driven snow, clean as a mountain stream, I'm strong now, I 'am vibrant now. All my organs and all my systems are functioning perfectly as the day I was born. My body eliminates what it needs to, assimilates what it needs to and circulates what it needs to. My body is the temple of the living spirit. Every part of my body is in harmony with that living spirit. It is forever renewed by that same spirit and I'm now made vigorous and whole. Every breath I draw is a breath of perfection, rebuilding and renewing every cell of my body. I possess the vitality of the Infinite, I'm strong and well. Many people would called me silly, childish and misguided, it's all just humanistic thinking but I have learned that the person that can carry the spirit of a child into adulthood, the optimism, the giddiness, the willingness to believe is not being childish at all, but a genius. That's where true belief springs from as silly as it sounds. Childlike belief. So at fifty years of age with graying temples I finally became a child prodigy.

Soul;   Even at a young age in life I intuitively knew that a real relationship with God was the most important possession a man could have. I went to church on Sunday's, read my Bible occasionally, tried to be a (quote unquote) good person to the best of my ability, but ironically it took the Grim Reaper and his bony fingers to show me how much deeper how much wider how much higher I could go. The heights, the breath, the depths and the widths of a relationship with God is immeasurable and inexhaustible and at that point in time in my life I realize I had only scratched the surface. I remembered the old adage; mighty oaks from little acorns grow, well it seemed to me my relationship with God was just a sapling. It was time to do some serious watering, serious pruning and grow this young root into the mighty oak it was always meant to be.

The teachings of Jesus Christ are truly an electric and dynamic gospel. Applying them to one's self makes the life history of that individual completely different from what it would have been without it. I can attest to that and more than likely so can all of us to some level I'm sure. With this miraculous knowledge life is to be met and mastered. Life's condition and outer appearances are simply of no importance in themselves except as they supply the materials needed for growth. You grow in grace and understanding by solving your daily problems as they arise. You are a child of the Most High you spring forth from a royal priesthood and a unique lineage. You are the very apple of God's eye, precious and priceless. That is who I am, that is who you are and the only real tragedy in life is when we suffer without ever learning the lesson that the suffering represents.

In dealing with my own sickness I grew spiritually by leaps and bounds. I attacked my problem from all angles. I aligned my spirit, my body, and my mind to the Creator who loves me, and God surely responded. My numbers (viral count) went from off the charts to almost undetectable within a year. I was ecstatic, very joyful and very thankful. God's power is potent to the extent of the faith we have in it. I was able to handle work easier, no more fevers, no more crippling fatigue, life became harmonious again and I couldn't have been more grateful. To know that God is, All Powerful, All Loving, All Forgiving is not sufficient, we must embody these qualities within ourselves before they can appear in our lives, we must seek to express them before they can take hold. Again I say either Jesus Christ meant what He said "That we can do all things through Him" or He didn't. I know He did and I stand here today as living proof.

The lessons I learned going through this personal ordeal of mine were quite priceless. I learned that we must engage all three aspects of our nature, Body, Mind and Soul to navigate this maze of life correctly. We must appreciate all that is around us big and small. Time isn't precious it's priceless. We must fire on all cylinders or we simply handicap ourselves in the middle of our race. I had still one more lesson one more course before I could close the book on this chapter in my life. That was patience and it can be the hardest lesson of all. (Isaiah 40:31) But they that wait upon the Lord shall renew their strength. They shall mount up with wings as eagles, they shall run and never weary, they shall walk and never faint).

It took over a year but my life finally stabilized my (so called) numbers my viral load went from well over a million to just four thousand, just a speck away from completely gone and in my mind I was healed. No fear, no fevers, no fatigue. I felt truly validated, for when I needed strength, it was there, when I needed hope, it was also there and when I needed some sort of closure it came just in the nick of time. One thing is for sure, God is going to teach you patience but in the midst of that patience, that waiting, there is a knowing an all soothing confidence that your affairs and ordeals are dear to the heart of the Lord and often times that's all you'll need.

I was healed in more ways than one for the word appreciation was forever etched in my heart. I take nothing for granted anymore, "This is the day the Lord hath made" and every day became a new day the Lord created just for me but in the midst of my joy and appreciation I was left with one tiny little thorn in my side. As happy and relieved as I was there still was the fact that my body did not eliminate the virus completely. I still had a minute amount of the virus in my system. It was no longer destroying my liver like it did but it was still there lurking. It wasn't making me sick like it used to, but it was still there, again leaving me a little confused. Why heal me most of the way and not all the way. Why must I have this little thorn in my side instead of being completely wiped clean. Jesus Christ in His day never healed anyone half way. Those people He healed did not have relapses, when Jesus would say "Go and suffer no more" He meant no more. So why am I still dealing with this. I was confused and sought counsel with many knowledgeable people on the subject. Most of them would point out the fact that the apostle Paul himself had a thorn in his side. Three times Paul asked the Lord to heal him and the Lords response was my grace is sufficient for thee. It seemed that even many of the people I spoke too had chronic ailments they could not overcome they gave up trying they gave up praying and would use this instance in Paul's life as some kind of excuse for not being able to vanquish their own personal thorn. This simply just did not wash with me and if Paul had a thorn he could not reverse it wasn't because God couldn't heal him there had to be another reason.

Paul's Two Thorns

I would like to preface this by saying that next to Jesus Christ Himself no one has done more to further the Christian movement than the apostle Paul himself. His writings and teachings are second to none and He is revered as one of the greatest souls to ever walk this planet. Paul's whole life was in service to God even when he was persecuting the Christians (Saul of Tarsus) he wholeheartedly thought he was doing God's work suppressing a counterfeit insurgency that was flaring up in the region. Paul was a Pharisee, top in his class, a real alpha dog but when he saw he was wrong he had the courage to admit it and go headlong over to the other side. I wonder how many people have ever realized what it must have cost Paul to come out in front of all his own people the Jews, where he held such a distinguished place and admit he was wrong. Paul's life is a study in man's quest for spiritual growth. Paul was not some kind of superman or anointed saint so that he had nothing in common with us. He was as human as human comes. He had a divine encounter with Christ himself but so can we, right here and right now. He dealt with all the same needs and wants as you and I have. He had great talents and he had great faults (sound familiar)? Early in his Christian life, before the Christ consciousness had completely illuminated him, Paul with all due respect was an utter and complete snob. He was completely full of himself. Keep in mind, he like we were just beginning to evolve as Christians but this imperfect disposition was most positively Paul's Thorn Number One. He was intensely proud of his Hebrew heritage. He descended from the tribe of Benjamin and thought all other Hebrews were a little inferior to him. He was not only a Benjamite but also a Pharisee and among that particular little group there was one chosen above all and that was Saul of Tarsus. To top it all off he was also a Roman Citizen and had full legal rights in the Roman Empire. At first he had a half conscious contempt for the Gentiles and seemed to relish keeping women in their place. I do not write this to smear Paul but to show you he was as human as you and I. He had a fault in his own disposition that would cause him terrible pain and suffering for a time but nothing could keep him off the spiritual path he was heading down. Nothing would keep him from his appointment with God not even his own frightful egotism. It seems as in Paul's case that the thing that brings us the most grief we seldom suspect or even recognize its there.

Paul's thorn in his side cannot be used as an excuse not to overcome something that is meant to be overcome. Period! Paul as incredible as he was is not my ultimate example, Jesus is and Jesus say's all things are possible. Jesus surmounted every kind of limitation to which mankind is subject. Jesus summed up the truth, taught it thoroughly and completely, but above all expressed it perfectly in his own life. Most importantly however he taught the science and the art of prayer and that prayer does change things, that prayer gets concrete results. Jesus in my life gets the final say he is my ultimate example.

So why wasn't the virus completely eliminated in my case? Why was that little thorn still in me? Why was Paul being the great healer of many still dealing with his? Let's find out.

(Paul's second thorn) Paul had founded the Corinthian church on his first visit. He was back there now for a third time countering all the false teachers and prophets that had influenced the Corinthians in his absence. He was being attacked and questioned about his authority as an Apostle of

Jesus Christ. False teachers were encouraging the believers to ignore Paul. Greece was known for its eloquent and persuasive orators. They had quite the speaking tour circuit and some were judging Paul comparing him to other speakers they had heard. Paul himself readily admits he is not eloquent of tongue.

Corinthian 11:5 Paul say's I do not think I am in the least bit inferior to those (super apostles). I may not be a trained speaker but I do have knowledge.

Paul believed in a simple presentation of the gospel, and some people thought this showed simple mindedness. Truth and content are far more important than presentation and delivery, but it shows how easily a person can be swayed by a silver tongue. So Paul sticking up for himself let loose about himself. Boasting because he felt he had to, he hit them with all his credentials and when he was done he probably felt a little embarrassed about his self-promotion. Here come the answer to why Paul couldn't get rid of his thorn.

He says in Corinthians (12:7) "To keep me from becoming conceited because of these surpassingly great revelations, there was given me a thorn in my flesh a messenger of Satan to torment me. Three times I pleaded with the Lord to take it away from me but He said to me, "My grace is sufficient for you for My power is made perfect in weakness. This is Paul's second thorn. Some have suggested that it was malaria, or epilepsy or a disease of the eyes. (see Galatians (4:13-15) whatever the case it was chronic and debilitating but more importantly it was in Paul's case needed. I repeat needed, needed to keep Paul humble. If it was not needed, (again in Paul's mind) to keep Paul humble it would have been removed when Paul originally asked. It is sad if a physical debilitation is needed to keep ones feet on the ground but if it is, it will remain. Paul's case is unique and not to be used as an example of why you might not be healed of whatever is troubling you. It's not the time for rationalizations. I do not need hepatitis to keep me humble or keep my feet on the ground. Hepatitis is not doing me any good and therefore I do not accept it and it will be overcome. In Pauls' unique case it seems whatever his ailment was he felt he needed it that somehow it was doing him some good. He said so in his own words "To keep me from becoming conceited there was given me a thorn in my flesh." My thorn I know is not needed and therefore I know it will be cured completely. We are to ask for strength when we are ill or weak but not strength to resign ourselves to inharmonious situations. Much of Paul's 1st thorn he overcame with maturity in Christ. His disposition improved considerably but as for his second thorn his physical ailment not much else is said, but if Paul truly felt he needed it as he stated then he was going to keep it one way or the other. I think Paul might have been taken aback at the way that the thorn in my side scripture has been used to resign ourselves to suffering. I do not believe he meant for that to happen for in his final greeting before leaving the Corinthians he says (Corinthians 13:11) "Finally brothers good bye. Aim for perfection, Aim for perfection, Wow. We cannot aim for perfection if we resign ourselves to anything less. I'm not saying that we will always get what we want but we most certainly will get what we need. Kind of sounds like a Rolling Stones song doesn't it. I wanted to be completely healed ten years ago. That's what I wanted. What I didn't know and the Lord did was that the doctors would come out with a new treatment down the road that was half the length of the original one with an 80 percent cure rate. That is tremendous news, that is a miracle and that is what I've been waiting for, even though I didn't know it all this time. "Those that wait upon the Lord shall have their strength renewed.

Those that wait upon the Lord shall FIRE ON ALL CYLINDERS